ALL OF

Glynn Christian's

ENTERTAINING MICROWAVE

ALL OF
Glynn
Christian's

ENTERTAINING
MICROWAVE

PRION

First published in Great Britain in 1995 by PRION
32-34 Gordon House Road,
London NW5 1LP

A catalogue record of this book can be obtained
from the British Library

ISBN 1-85375-204-5

Typeset in 11/12 Stone Serif by
Books Unlimited (Nottm), Mansfield NG19 7QZ

Printed in Great Britain by
Biddles Ltd., Guildford & Kings Lynn

Contents

Vegetables and vegetarian

Fish and seafood

Poultry and meat

Puddings

A concise introduction to microwave cooking

Microwave cookery is fast, safe and clean; a combination that has benefits for everyone. The principles are simple, learning to use it perfectly straightforward, and you do not necessarily need to buy new cookery equipment to get good results.

But like every other piece of new equipment and technology in your house, it does require an initial investment of time to ensure you understand how it works and thus how it can work best for you.

The most important thing to get clear in your mind is that microwave cooking is a wet method, essentially steaming, and that more often than not the steam is produced by the liquid contained in the food being cooked. So food is initially likely to become wetter rather than drier. But once the moisture is driven off, the food will dry as it would in conventional cooking, sometimes an advantage, sometimes not. Any claim that microwave food is intrinsically dry is quite wrong; if microwaved food is dry it's as a result of overcooking.

Microwaves are a type of radio wave that have the ability to excite the molecules of liquids, fats and oils, and sugar. They jiggle the molecules against each other over two billion times a second, and that friction is what creates the internal heat. That turns water into steam or heats the fat, oil or sugar, and the food cooks. It is absolutely wrong to think microwaves in some way break down the cells or structure of food; it is the cookery process which does that, as in any other form of cookery.

The reason for the exceptional speed of much microwave cookery is that the microwaves penetrate food to about 4 cm (1½") and are thus cooking the food to that depth at the same time. Conventional methods first heat the outside and then slowly conduct heat towards the centre; so microwave cooking has more than a head start.

Unless there is a very high fat content, microwaving is unlikely to brown food, simply because of the steam produced, and it is best not to expect browning, just as you would not expect a poacher or steamer to do so.

The rules about covering food in a microwave are simple: if you would cover it in conventional methods, cover it in the microwave – covering basically helps retain moisture, and this can be particularly important in microwaving as some moisture is being driven out of the food by the cooking/steaming process. On the other hand I find many microwave cookbooks concentrate more on such techniques than on decent recipes, with witless instructions to cook vegetables in plastic bags, wrap everything else in cling film, wrap foil around chicken legs, and so on and so on. Most of this is silly, self-important posturing, often to sell some product or another. A plate over a bowl, or a plate inverted on another plate is usually more than enough, both simpler and cheaper to use than cling film, and you also create a warm plate upon which to serve food. Incidentally, plates and bowls which come from a microwave feeling hot do so because the food has passed heat to them: they have not been heated by microwaves as they do not contain liquid, fat or sugar.

You should also be suspicious of instructions to wrap foil over thinner parts of, say, poultry, on the basis that this prevents such parts overcooking. Thinner parts of a bird cook faster in conventional methods and you don't waste time or money preventing this. Why should microwave be different? Such over-complicated techniques defeat the principle attraction of microwave cooking – its speed.

Even the most expensive conventional oven can have cool spots, and so do microwave cookers. This is because the energy is created at a single source and bounced around the inside of the cooker. You will quickly establish where these parts are in your cooker, and learn to compensate. The best advice I can give is always to cook food on a microwave-safe trivet or support of some kind, so that microwaves can be bounced from the floor of the cooker into the base of the container. This helps ensure more even cooking, and is essential with dense or large amounts of food. When cooking small amounts of food, moving the cooking container during cooking is a bore and often unnecessary, particularly if a trivet is used. But you will find it vital when cooking something as dense as a bread pudding. The single most important rule to help even cooking is that ingredients should be arranged towards the outside of any container, with the thicker parts to the outside and thinner pointing inwards. Wherever possible food should be the same size or density.

Remember also that the more liquid there is, the more microwave power is used and the longer it will take for something to cook. Thus for soups or casserole type dishes, you should start the dish with as little liquid as possible, only adding the full amount towards the end. Poaching liquid for fish or fruit will not have the time to reduce in quantity, so use less and flavour it more highly.

Resting food after cooking is eminently good sense with all cooking. The resting time helps even the temperature of the food, and in the case of fish, poultry and meat allows the flesh to relax and reabsorb the juices, becoming more tender and moist. But, because the difference between the outer and inner temperatures of microwave cooked food may be greater, you should be a little more assiduous in resting it. In most cases, the time you take to serve the food is enough.

Pyrex and related glass ceramic products are amongst the best types of kitchen ware for microwave cooking, particularly as most people have them anyway. But it is certainly worth looking to see what is now specially made for microwave cookery. Glass and ceramic products do absorb and hold the heat created in the food: if you want to keep vegetables hot this is an advantage, but if you have baked a cake, the retained heat continues to dry the mixture as it cools. The range of thin white microwave-safe cookware is cheap and often extremely innovative and useful. Cake mixtures always cook more evenly in a ring mould and if you have one of these you can serve a fruit upside-down steamed pudding in 4 to 5 minutes. But things are moving on. A Canadian company has perfected the Micro-Mac range, using a clear material which lets virtually all the microwaves through to the food and absorbs very little of the heat back. This means cooking time can be reduced even more, often by as much as 20 per cent. Worth watching out for.

Nothing metal, containing metal or with metallic decoration should be used in a microwave cooker. But sometimes the metal is concealed. To test a container's suitability, stand it in the microwave with a glass of water inside it. Put the microwave on High for 2 minutes or so. If there is any arcing turn off the cooker at once, as this is a sign of metal content. If not, continue and when the time is up, compare the temperature of the water and the container you are testing. If the container is safe, the water will be hot and the container cool. If the water is cool or the container hot, the container has been deflecting or absorbing the microwaves and is unsuitable for use.

Frankly, most of the essential information you need is in the instruction book which comes with your cooker – but we are all guilty of never reading these. Once you get rid of false expectations, no longer believe microwaves cook from the inside out, stop thinking you need special equipment or to wrap everything in cling film, there is a wonderfully simple and delicious world of microwave cookery to be enjoyed.

I hope my Entertaining Microwave series and recipes help you to discover it.

Recently, microwave cookers have had their power ratings reassigned, for reasons best known only to a few – and they aren't telling. Essentially all you need to know is that what used to be called a 750-watt cooker is now an 850-watt, and that is considered the fundamental microwave these days. However as individual cookers can vary as much as 50 watts or more in power the supposed differences are often academic. Just as you would with any new piece of kitchen or cooking equipment, watch carefully when you first use your microwave and judge for yourself; does it give faster or slower results than it should? Whatever the answer, this is the way you adapt and adopt when you cook.

The microwave cooker used throughout the series was new-rated 850 watt power and has 9 power levels. PL9 is High and thus PL5 is the equivalent of Medium on other cookers, and PL7 is Medium High. To adjust these recipes for cookers of different powers, use the following tables as a broad guide: if your machine is older, remember that 750 watts on this chart also refers to a machine rated 650 by the old system.

750 watts: add 5 seconds per minute
700 watts: add 10 seconds per minute
650 watts: add 15 seconds per minute
600 watts: add 20 seconds per minute

But don't be baffled by charts. Please remember that all recipes are only a guide, not a formula to be followed precisely and guaranteeing exact results. The density and shape of food to be microwaved, the way you arrange it, the cleanliness of your cooker and personal preference all play their part. It's really only small pieces of delicate, very fatty or very sweet foods which need real care as they attract a high density of micro-wave; otherwise there is leeway, as there is with all types of cookery.

The microwave cooker and much advice was provided by AEG Domestic Appliances, for which Glynn Christian wishes to record his grateful thanks.

Soups and salads

Chilled tomato and gin soup

You can't easily cook with gin, as its flavour is very fugitive. But use it to finish this soup which uses many of gin's basic flavourings and you really get something to start the meal right.

Serves 6

1.5kg/3lb really ripe tomatoes, plum or roma variety
200g/6oz onion, finely chopped
2 tablespoons vegetable oil
1 teaspoon coriander seeds, lightly crushed
1 teaspoon juniper berries, lightly crushed
1 teaspoon black pepper corns, lightly crushed
2 fresh bay leaves, torn
thinly pared skin of a small orange
salt to taste
150ml/¼ pint gin (or more) ice cold
1 or 2 cartons soured cream
6 tablespoons cucumber, coarsely chopped

Combine the onion, oil, crushed spices, bay leaves and orange peel in a large ovenproof bowl, cover with a plate and cook on High for 4–5 minutes, until the onion is really tender. Meanwhile roughly chop the tomatoes, reserving all the juice. Add to the prepared mixture, stir well, cover and microwave until just boiling, about 5–6 minutes, stirring 2 or 3 times. Don't cook too long or the tomato will lose its colour. Purée and sieve, using the back of a soup ladle rather than a wooden spoon to ensure maximum yield. Cover and chill, and then salt to your taste.

To serve, ladle into flat rather than deep bowls, which are better for being chilled. Into each roughly stir 1½ tablespoons or more of iced gin: it does not have to be evenly mixed in. Put a dollop of soured cream in the middle of each and top with the chopped cucumber, a vital part of the flavour affinities.

Chilled pea soup with blue cheese and lemon cream

Lightly crumbled blue cheese adds a fascinating, salty tang to vegetables and soups. Here its colour, texture and flavour are part of the finish of a simple-to-make pea soup, and yes, frozen peas are best. You can use mint instead of dill, but I find it so easily overpowers the delicacy of peas: equally, leek is kinder than onions. An outstandingly good picnic soup, refreshing but robust and piquant when transported cold and finished as you serve.

Serves 6

750g/1½lb frozen petits pois, defrosted
200g/6oz white of leek, finely sliced
2 teaspoons water
3 tablespoons parsley, coarsely chopped
1 tablespoon dill, coarsely chopped
1.2 litres/2 pints chicken or vegetable stock, chilled
300ml/½ pint soured cream
1 lemon
200g/6oz firm blue cheese, chopped or crumbled

Combine the peas, leeks, water and two herbs, cover and cook on High for about 5 minutes, stirring a couple of times, but do not let the peas overcook and lose their brilliant colour. Quickly pour on half the stock, which will prevent further cooking. Liquidise and sieve, using the back of a soup ladle rather than a wooden spoon to ensure maximum yield.

Stir in the remaining stock, straining if need be, cover and chill. Add extra stock to get a smooth, even texture: only salt lightly, if at all, as the blue cheese will provide this.

To serve, grate the zest of the lemon directly into the soured cream and fold together. Serve the soup, add a dollop of the lemon cream and sprinkle with the blue cheese. Some chopped parsley or a dill frond would do no harm.

Chicken and corn soup

Said to be the world's single most popular Chinese dish.

Serves 4

   3–4 large cobs fresh corn
   or
   350g/12oz drained canned corn
   1.2 litres/2 pints chicken stock
   2 boneless chicken breasts, minced
   2 egg whites, lightly beaten
   2 teaspoons light soy sauce
   1 tablespoon cornflour
   2 tablespoons water

Slice the kernels from the corn cobs, reserving as much of the juice as possible. If you have more than you need, keep them to use as a garnish for the cooked soup. Mix the egg whites and the soy into the minced or processed chicken. Using a deep bowl or large measuring jug, heat cold stock for 4 minutes on High (or crumble one or two chicken stock cubes in 1.2 litres/2 pints water and heat for the same amount of time). Add the corn and cook on High for 3 minutes; for canned corn cook on High for 1 minute.

Mix the cornflour with the water, stir in and cook for 1 minute on High. Now mix in the chicken and cook at PL5/Medium for 6–10 minutes, stirring a couple of times to break up the chicken. Serve with a little Chinese vinegar or chilli sauce, perhaps a sprinkle of coriander leaf and any raw corn kernels you might have.

Proper onion soup

Reputedly one of the world's greatest pick-me-ups, so simple but very time consuming to make properly. The microwave cuts the time in half and gives better results.

Serves 4 – 6

50g/2oz butter
1kg/2lb onions, finely sliced
2 teaspoons sugar
900ml (2 cans) beef consommé
150ml white wine or water
4 tablespoons cognac
Optional: toasted French bread rounds
and grated Gruyère cheese

This amount of onion would normally take well over an hour first to soften and then turn sweet before browning. Put the onion (I slice mine in a food processor) into a large casserole with the butter, cover, and then cook on High for 10 minutes. Remove the lid, stir, arrange the onions in a doughnut shape and then continue to cook for another 20 minutes uncovered, stirring from time to time. Sprinkle on the sugar and stir in. Continue cooking for up to 10 minutes more or until the onions are nicely browning; they will be uneven but this is usual.

Add the wine or water and the stock, and stir well to untangle the onion. Add salt to taste, but not so much that you cover the sweetness which has taken so long to develop. Cover and cook for 5 minutes on High. Stir in the cognac just before serving from the casserole at the table.

Serving it with cheese-crusted toasts in the bowls is only one way of serving this soup and a bit of a bore to do: it's just as correct to toast some slices of French bread and to serve them separately as a dipper, with or without some Gruyère cheese to sprinkle on. I like a sprinkle of parsley too.

Borscht with beer

Not the smooth, clear, elegant version of grand restaurants, but a chunky vegetarian version: the beefing up of the flavour comes from beer instead.

Serves 4–6

125g/4oz onion, sliced finely
2 tablespoons oil
500g/1lb raw beetroot, chopped
125g/4oz celery, chopped
125g/4oz carrot, chopped
2 garlic cloves, finely chopped
2 tablespoons tomato purée
1 tablespoon cider or wine vinegar
900ml/1½ pints beer
250g/8oz green cabbage, finely shredded or
   sliced
300ml/½ pint water or stock
salt, pepper and sugar to taste
chopped parsley, soured cream and lemon
   wedges to serve

Cook the onions in the oil for 5 minutes or more on High whilst you assemble or prepare the other ingredients. It won't hurt if they brown just a little. Stir in the beetroot, celery, carrot, garlic, tomato purée, vinegar and half the beer. Cover and cook on High for 5–10 minutes or until the vegetables are cooked: this will depend on their size and evenness. Now add the rest of the beer and the cabbage, stir very well and cook for another 5–10 minutes until the cabbage is cooked but like the other vegetables retains a slight bite. It is worth stirring them from time to time to ensure even cooking.

   To proceed, add the water or stock and heat through for 5 minutes on High. Now season with salt and pepper: if the bitterness of the beer is too extreme for your palate, add sugar in small amounts, only a teaspoon at a time, as the effect is dramatic. Like all soups, the borscht will be better for being allowed to stand. Reheat when you are ready to serve. Top each bowl full with chopped parsley, and then add soured cream and a generous wedge of lemon for squeezing in as you eat.

Chili-corn tomato soup with chorizo and tostados

Based on Mexican flavours, this is warming in winter but welcome in summer as a light meal with zing.

Serves up to 6

   zest of large sweet orange
   100g/4oz onion, chopped
   2 or 3 cloves garlic, chopped
   1 stick celery, finely sliced
   1 bay leaf
   2 teaspoons chili powder, medium or hot
   1kg/2lb ripe red tomatoes
   1 can sweet corn, creamed or kernels

Zest the orange directly into the bottom of a large casserole. Add the onion, garlic, celery, bay and chili powder: note this must be chili (a mixture of spices) and not chilli, which is only cayenne pepper. Stir, cover and cook for 5 minutes on High. Meanwhile, remove stalks from tomatoes and chop roughly, reserving all the liquid. Add to the casserole, cover and cook on High for 15 minutes, stirring once or twice.

Now you have some choices: for a peasanty look, add the corn to this mixture, heat through and serve.

For more elegance, liquidise and sieve: you don't have to be too assiduous about the puréeing but it is a help. Now stir in the corn, heat on High for a few minutes and serve. Creamed corn gives a silkier finish. For even more bulk add a few slices of chorizo sausage.

Squeeze in a wedge of lime before serving with tostados.

Note: you can use corn freshly scraped from the kernels, in which case add to the tomato and cook on High for 5 minutes

Tostados/Nachos

Call them what you will (I call them both, I know) these are simply tortilla chips with added flavour. On each chip dab a small portion of jalapeño peppers, which are available in bottles and cans, a dab of chilli sauce and a sprinkle of grated cheese – Double Gloucester is just right. A couple of dozen spread over a large plate will be heated through and have nice melty cheese in only 40 seconds on High.

My minestrone

By adding both beans and pasta and finishing with fresh parsley and celery leaf, this becomes anything but classic yet couldn't have been developed without the traditions of minestrone.

Serves 6 or more

   8 tablespoons rich olive oil
   250g/8oz onion, finely sliced
   100g/4oz rindless bacon, chopped
   4 garlic cloves, sliced
   250g/8oz celery, sliced
   1kg/2lb mixed vegetables: see method
   400g can chopped tomatoes
   400g can cannelini beans, drained
   50g/2oz dried pasta shapes
   600ml/1 pint water or stock

To serve: olive oil; chopped parsley and celery leaf; freshly grated Parmesan cheese

Put the olive oil and prepared onion, bacon and garlic into a large casserole. Cover and cook on High for 8 minutes; the onion should be soft and the bacon rendered. Add the celery, other vegetables and the contents of the can of tomatoes and then stir. I use about 250g/8oz of each of four other vegetables, especially leeks, fennel, celeriac, courgettes and carrots, and cut each into different shapes. Cook on High for 10 minutes.

Mash half the beans and then stir those and the whole beans into the vegetables. Mix in the pasta shapes, add the water, and stir. Cook covered for 15 minutes or until the pasta is really soft. Season now if you must and cook longer if you like mushy vegetables. Serve in deep bowls: stir in chopped parsley and celery leaf and sprinkle on olive oil. Pass the cheese. Even better next day, of course.

Avocado chowder with warm chicken salad

I discovered the basis of this rich dish in Israel, where they are always inventing new ways to use up ripe avocados. It's very gratifying to eat.

Serves 6 or more

2 chicken legs (thighs and drumsticks)
250g/8oz onion, sliced
3 garlic cloves
50g/2oz fresh coriander or parsley
25g/1oz fresh ginger, chopped
1 lime
1 teaspoon salt
600ml/1 pint water or white wine
750g/1½lb avocado flesh plus 1 avocado

For salad:
100g/4oz tomato, chopped
15g/½ oz ginger, chopped
25g/1oz fresh coriander, roughly chopped
juice of a lime

Slash the chicken legs deeply to the bone all over and arrange evenly in the bottom of a casserole. Add the onion, garlic, coriander or parsley, and ginger. Slice the lime, skin and all, and then add that with the salt and water or wine. Cover and cook on High for 20 minutes, stirring once or twice. Leave to stand at least an hour to develop flavour further. Tip into a colander over a bowl and drain well. Reserve the stock and the legs but discard the remaining flavourings.

Take the skin from the legs and chop or cut the flesh into strips. Cover.

For the required amount of avocado flesh you will need to buy about 1.5kg/3lbs in weight of ripe avocados. Put one aside. Scoop out the flesh of the others, including the green lining of the skins. Purée this and whisk into the stock. Press cling film to the surface and it will keep without discolouring for several hours.

When you are ready to serve, cover and reheat the soup for about 5 minutes – don't let it boil too long. Meanwhile dice the flesh of the remaining avocado and squeeze on the lime juice. Sprinkle the chicken with the ginger and toss lightly with the avocado and lime juice. Add plenty of black pepper. Heat on High for 1 minute and then mix with the coriander and tomato.

Serve the soup into flat soup bowls and pile the warm chicken salad in the middle.

Warm macadamia-mustard goat cheese with chilli-mint sauce

A classic modern dish with an Australian twist.

Serves 2 as a substantial first course or light main course

> 2 fresh but firm individual goat cheeses (usually 100g each)
> 50g/2oz macadamia nuts, chopped
> 2 tablespoons best quality seed mustard
> 2 or 3 teaspoons Oriental chilli sauce
> 4–6 fresh mint leaves

Arrange the chopped macadamia nuts in a ring on a flat plate and microwave on High for 1½ minutes. Mix lightly, rearrange into the doughnut shape and cook for a further 30 seconds or more, just until the first nut begins to brown. Allow to cool a little and then mix with the seed mustard to make a mixture which holds together – the amount of mustard will depend on how finely you have chopped the nuts. Divide the mixture into two, make a hole in the middle of each pile the same size as each cheese, and stand the cheeses there. Use a teaspoon and then the flat of a knife blade to pat and push the mixture firmly around the sides of the cheeses, letting a small amount tumble over the top, for the sake of rusticity. If you have the time let them sit at room temperature for an hour which will greatly enhance the flavour.

Prepare an interesting salad of mixed leaves and dress lightly with a nut oil – walnut or hazelnut – and a little good vinegar. Pile high on individual plates. Finely slice or chop the mint leaves and mix into an oriental chilli sauce, one of the sweet but hot ones you can use like a ketchup.

Microwave the two cheeses together on Medium for 2½ minutes or until the cheeses are JUST warm to the touch. Use a spatula to put a warm cheese on each salad, top with the prepared sauce.

May be served without the salad or with just a small salad garnish.

Artichoke and potato with prawns and walnuts

Fast food with an earthy flavour direct from the store cupboard and freezer. Great as a first course, satisfying as a main course.

Serves 2 as a maincourse, 6 as a first course

400g can small potatoes
400g can artichoke hearts
50g/2oz walnuts, halved
250g/8oz or more mixed cooked seafood
3 tablespoons walnut oil
1 tablespoon balsamic or sherry vinegar
zest of a lime or lemon

Spread the walnuts on a flat plate and microwave on High for 2 minutes: stir, check and cook more to get an even colour.

Cut the potatoes and the artichokes into quarters

and gently mix. Microwave on High for 2 minutes. Whilst warm, mix together 3 tablespoons of walnut oil and about 1 of vinegar. Sprinkle over the salad and mix through, being careful not to break up the vegetables. Turn the seafood on to that and scatter with the warm walnuts. Zest the lime or lemon directly on to that and serve at once.

Lentil and sausage salad

Gratifying enough to be a main course. If you have vegetarians to serve, leave out the sausage and offer it separately.

Serves 6 or more

> 2 x 400g cans cooked green lentils, drained
> 150g/6oz smoked garlic sausage, sliced
> 100g/4oz pickled cucumber or gherkins
> 25g/1oz onion, chopped
> 1 garlic clove, crushed
> 8 tablespoons vegetable oil (safflower or
>   sunflower)
> 4 tablespoons cider or wine vinegar
> 2 tablespoons whole grain mustard
> 1 teaspoon caraway seeds
> salt and pepper

Heat the lentils until hot for up to 3 minutes on High: gently mix in the sausage and cucumber.

In a small bowl, mix together the onion, garlic, oil and vinegar, cover and heat on High for 1 minute. Meanwhile, stir the caraway seeds and mustard into the warm lentil and sausage mixture.

Strain the hot vinaigrette over the mixture, toss lightly and serve with plenty of bread. If you like the sliced sausage can be gently warmed through in the microwave before being added to the salad.

Chicken liver and buttered apples on wilted bitter salad

The butter and cognac act as the oil and vinegar you would normally expect, and their sweetness is counteracted by the bite of the wilted greens. Outstandingly good as a lunch with plenty of bread and wine.

Serves 2–4

250g/8oz chicken livers
4 tablespoons cognac or armagnac
2 Golden Delicious apples, peeled, cored and
  segmented
50g/2oz butter
50g/2oz each watercress and rocket leaves

Gently prick the chicken livers (to avoid exploding) arrange in a single layer and pour over the cognac or armagnac. Pick the salads (removing the stalks of the watercress), wash, dry and toss together in a serving bowl. Keep cool but not refrigerated.

Put the apple segments into a suitable container, dot with the butter and cook on High for up to 5 minutes, when they will be cooked but still firm. Cover to keep hot. Cook the livers, covered lightly, on PL7/Medium High for 2 minutes, season lightly and then allow to rest a few minutes by which time they will be slightly pink in the centre and deliciously tender and juicy. To serve, tip the hot apples and chicken livers on to the salad and toss well, which makes the leaves wilt and turn a brighter green. Their bitter bite will probably mean you won't want to add pepper.

Warm scallop salad with a blueberry vinaigrette

Great autumnal colours and flavours with a mustardy bite to balance the fabulous sweetness of scallops. The salad can first be dressed lightly with oil and a special vinegar, as long as this does nothing more than lightly coat the leaves. But you can use just the fruit vinaigrette.

Serves 2 as a main course, 4 as a first course

> 250g/8oz scallops, including corals if possible
> 250g/8oz blueberries, blackberries or raspberries
> 1 tablespoon made mustard (not English)
> 4 tablespoons vegetable oil
> 2 tablespoons cider vinegar
> salt and pepper
> prepared salad leaves

Prepare the scallops by carefully removing the coral, then the thin membrane which surrounds each white part, and then the tough, whiter muscle that sits on one side. Turn each prepared scallop on to its side and cut in half, across the grain. Arrange these and the corals in a single layer and cover lightly. A scatter of fruity or sweet white wine or of cognac does no harm.

Ideally the salad leaves should include some of those with an autumnal touch to their edges, but do not include the bright red radicchio. Use plenty of them and you have something substantial; serve just a handful and you have an elegant, lighter first course or main meal. Arrange the salad on a large flat plate, or on serving plates, giving the leaves plenty of centre height.

Put the fruit and mustard into a food processor and whiz until smooth: with the motor still running, add the oil and then the vinegar. Taste and season. Spoon over the salad. Cook the scallops for 45 seconds on High, just enough to warm them through. Salt lightly and distribute evenly over the salad.

Vegetables and vegetarian

Concentrated plum tomatoes

1kg/2lb ripe but firm plum tomatoes

Arrange evenly in a deep microwave-safe dish and pierce each tomato from top to bottom with a sharp knife, but do not cut through the bottom skin. Cook at PL2 for up to 3 hours tipping away excess liquid from time to time. They will eventually shrivel and you will see some of the juices just begin to caramelise: the exact degree of concentration is up to you.

To serve as a first course, put one or two concentrated tomatoes on a small plate with a generous slice of buffalo-milk mozzarella. Drizzle on extra virgin olive oil and a little balsamic vinegar and garnish with fresh herbs.

Chilli and lemon grass sweet potato cake

This is especially good using pink sweet potatoes, but white ones or ordinary potatoes are just as acceptable.

Serves 4

750g/1½lb sweet potatoes
6 small bulb ends only, lemon grass
2.5cm/1" fresh ginger, peeled
1 or 2 fresh red chillies, deseeded
1 fresh lime
1 tablespoon water
1 teaspoon salt

Peel the potatoes, putting them into acidulated water as you go so they do not darken and discolour. Slice medium thin, perhaps using the thicker option of a food processor, and return to the water. Bruise the lemon grass bulbs, removing any central woodiness you might discover. Put them into a processor with the ginger and chilli. Zest or grate the peel of the lime directly into this and then squeeze in the juice. Add the water and salt. Process until finely chopped.

Drain the potatoes, toss in the processed mixture and arrange evenly in a microwave-safe dish just deep enough to hold them. Cover loosely with cling film and cook on High for 9 minutes. As soon as they come from the cooker, rest three or four plates on the potatoes, without removing the cling film, to press them tightly. They will remain hot for hours; otherwise make in advance and reheat on High for 3 minutes – longer if they have been refrigerated. Turn out on to a platter, garnish with something suitable, and serve in wedges. Good with fresh lime squeezed over each serving.

Stuffed onions

Sweetened by the microwave and stuffed with a Middle Eastern style rice, this converts the humble onion into a real treat.

Serves 6 as a first course

   3 large onions, about 150g/6oz each
   100g/4oz cooked rice
   50g/2oz dried apricots, sliced
   25g/1oz butter
   ½ teaspoon ground cumin
   2 teaspoons mint leaves, chopped
   15g/½oz currants
   15g/½oz pine kernels
   thick yoghurt, ground cumin and mint sprigs to
     serve

Peel each onion but leave all the root attached. Cook covered for 10 minutes or more on High until nicely tender and sweet. Cut each onion through from top to bottom and remove everything except the outer three layers. Chop the onion you have removed and mix with the rice, butter, apricots, cumin, mint, currants and pine kernels – in fact the proportions are unimportant and you can play to make a combination you like. Stuff evenly into the onion shells and cook uncovered on High for 7 minutes or until piping hot.

Serve with a dollop of yoghurt, a sprinkle of cumin and a sprig of mint.

Spinach frittata

The flat omelette of the Mediterranean has many names, but nothing is more delicious when just lukewarm or cold. It usually takes forever to cook in a slow oven, but the microwave does it in less than 15 minutes.

Serves 4–6

750g/1½ lb potatoes, peeled, sliced
2 tablespoons olive oil
6 eggs
250g/8oz chopped spinach, drained weight

Turn the prepared potatoes in the olive oil and arrange evenly in a flat shallow container, about 20cm/9" across. Cover with a plate and cook on High for 8 minutes. Ensure the spinach is well drained and squeezed. Mix with the eggs and pour over the potatoes. Agitate gently to ensure even distribution. Cook on High uncovered for 8 minutes. Allow to sit until lukewarm and serve with extra virgin olive oil as a sauce.

Dry potato curry

Sometimes it's good to turn the tables and to serve a curried vegetable with plain meat, poultry or fish. This recipe for potatoes can be used with other root vegetables, or with a mixture which makes a good main course for vegetarians.

Serves 6 as an accompaniment

> 1.25kg/3lb potatoes, peeled
> 1 tablespoon vegetable oil
> 250g/8oz onion, finely chopped
> ½ teaspoon cumin seed
> ½ teaspoon coriander seed, crushed
> 150ml/¼ pint stock or water
> 2 teaspoons curry paste or powder, or to taste
> 3 – 4 tablespoons lemon or lime juice
> few pinches red pepper flakes (optional)

The potatoes should be cut into cubes of about 2.5cm/1". Mix together the oil, onions, spices, curry paste and pepper flakes. Cook on High for 3 minutes to develop the flavour and then stir in the potatoes, stock and citrus juice. Cover with a plate and cook on High for 15 minutes or until the potatoes are tender – it will depend on how large or small the pieces are. There should be very little or no liquid left, and what there is will be absorbed as you serve. Allow to stand for 3 or more minutes before doing so.

Braised Mediterranean vegetable medley

Provided each vegetable is about the same size and density you can use almost any that you like, but go for the exotic ones for the best effect.

Serves 4–6

1kg/2lb vegetables – see method
olive oil
50g/2oz Parmesan cheese, cubed
25g/1oz flat parsley, roughly chopped

The vegetables I used were fennel bulbs, cut into quarters, chunks of butternut pumpkin, big pieces of yellow pepper and quartered fresh artichokes. To prepare the latter cut off about 7/8 of the top of the artichoke and discard; cut off the stalk to within 2cm/½" of the base.

Use a very sharp knife to trim the outer skin of the bottom scales of the artichoke back to the more tender insides. Now quarter the prepared artichoke and scoop out the hairy centre. Plunge into acidulated water until ready to proceed. Mix the vegetables with plenty of olive oil plus as much sliced garlic as you dare. Cover with a plate and cook on High for 15 minutes, perhaps stirring once if you have the inclination. Tip in the Parmesan cubes and the flat parsley, toss and serve. Wonderful cold, too.

Garlic-olive oil mash

When potatoes and other root vegetables are microwaved without added liquid, they come out of the cooker ready to mash.

Serves 4–6

1kg/2lb floury potatoes – King Edwards are the
  best
8 or more garlic cloves, sliced
(up to) 150ml/¼ pint olive oil

Peel the potatoes and cut into quarters. Mix with the prepared garlic in a large casserole in which they can lie in a single layer. Do not add any liquid. Cover and cook on High for 12 minutes. The potatoes should be cooked through and beginning to break up and dry a little. Mash by hand, slowly incorporating as much olive oil as you like. Salt to taste.

Roasted hot and sweet nuts

Whole almonds, cashew or macadamia nuts are particularly good like this.

250g/8oz blanched whole almonds
1 scant tablespoon clear honey
1 teaspoon vegetable oil
1 teaspoon sesame oil
(up to) 1 teaspoon chilli or chili powder
1 teaspoon garam masala
1 teaspoon ground ginger

Arrange the almonds in a hollow ring shape on a flat plate and microwave on High for 2 minutes. Mix thoroughly, rearrange and cook another minute or until only very lightly browned. Mix together the honey, oil and spices. Chilli is just ground chilli peppers or cayenne, but chili also contains such spices as cumin giving a broader spectrum of flavour and a choice of mild, medium or hot mixtures. Add to the warm nuts, stir well, rearrange in the ring shape and microwave on High for 4 minutes, stirring the mixture at least once.

Turn out on to non-stick baking paper to cool. Separate before serving cold. Best eaten the day they are made as they will go sticky.

Baby aubergine on minted peppers and leeks

A special vegetable dish for a special dinner, but also good as a first course, perhaps served warm as a crostini.

Serves 6

250g/8oz baby aubergines (6–8)
350g/12oz leeks, trimmed weight
350g/12oz yellow or orange peppers, trimmed
 weight
2 cloves garlic, chopped
25g/1oz butter
4 tablespoons olive oil
juice of up to half a lemon
30 mint leaves, plus garnish
50g/2oz fetta cheese, crumbled
extra virgin olive oil to finish

Leave the green stalks on the aubergines. Cut thinly up to the stem of each aubergine. Hold apart lightly and sprinkle the cut surfaces with a little salt. Leave to drain for 30 minutes.

Meanwhile, cut the leeks in quarters lengthways (in eighths if they are thick ones) and then into lengths of about 10cm/4". Rinse. Chop the peppers roughly. Mix with the leeks and the garlic, spread on the base of a flat bottomed casserole with a lid. Dot the vegetables with the butter, pour on the olive oil, lightly salt and pepper, toss and redistribute. Cook covered on High for 10 minutes. Slice the mint leaves and stir through evenly. Squeeze in a little lemon juice to sharpen the flavour but do not swamp the mint.

Rinse the drained aubergine and arrange evenly around the outside edge of the casserole on the cooked vegetables, with their stalks towards the centre. Cook covered on High for 5 minutes or until the aubergines are tender. They must be allowed to cool until only just warm to be most enjoyable.

Serve each aubergine on a bed of the other vegetables. Sprinkle with fetta cheese, pour on some richly flavoured extra virgin olive oil and pop on a sprig of mint for garnish.

Specially good served on warm crostini – thick slices of decent white bread scraped with garlic, drizzled with olive oil and lightly toasted.

Alsatian courgette ribbons

Prettier than a picture and with a dressing that offers the fascinating contrast of sweet dried pears, smoky bacon and the citric bite of toasted cumin seeds, all great favourites of Alsatian cooks. Serve with plainly cooked or roasted meat, fish or poultry.

Serves 4–6

750g/1½lb courgettes
1 generous teaspoon cumin seeds
50g/2oz dried pears
100g/4oz smoked streaky bacon
4 tablespoons fruity white wine
4 tablespoons cider vinegar
seasoning if required

Cut the courgettes into long ribbons, using a vegetable peeler. Toast the cumin seeds on a flat plate in the microwave on High for 1 to 2 minutes until they smell strongly and have gained a little colour. Mix into the courgettes, being careful not to break the ribbons.

Slice the pears and the bacon into thin strips. On a small plate with a rim, first lay the pears and then cover them with the bacon strips. Cook uncovered on High until the bacon has rendered its fat and is crisp – up to 7 minutes on High. Allow to rest, covered.

Sprinkle the courgettes with the white wine and cook uncovered on High. The time will be a matter of personal preference, but for crisp courgettes, 5 minutes will be enough; more than 8 minutes is likely to see them losing their colour. Once they are ready, reheat the bacon and pear mixture for just 1 minute on High, pour the cider vinegar on to them and turn that on to the courgettes, collecting any crustiness as you go. Toss lightly and serve.

Wicked sweet potatoes

A choice here. Serve the sweet potatoes with their syrupy sauce, or mash the mixture with dark rum and cream for the ultimate calorie and flavour treat. The pink-fleshed varieties look more festive, but white sweet potatoes will taste just as good.

Serves 4–6

   1kg/2lb sweet potatoes
   juice of 1 orange
   1 teaspoon allspice or cinnamon
   1 heaped tablespoon muscavado sugar
   50g/2oz butter
   4 tablespoons dark rum
   142ml/¼ pint carton double cream

Choose thinner rather than thicker sweet potatoes if you can. Peel and cut into rounds about 2.5cm/1" thick. Arrange evenly on a flat baking dish with a lip. Pour on the orange juice evenly, sprinkle on the spice and the sugar and then dot with the butter. Cook uncovered on High for about 10 minutes or until the potatoes are tender (they cook faster than ordinary potatoes); it is worthwhile basting them from time to time with the sauce which forms.

   If you would like to serve them as a wicked mash, first break them up then whisk. Once they are quite smooth, beat in the cream and rum and then season to taste.

Chinese stuffed cabbage leaves

Warming winter food which can be made even more substantial by the inclusion of sliced ham or cubed tofu.

Serves 3-4 as a main course, more as a first course or in a buffet or Chinese-style meal

> 6 large cabbage leaves,
> 1 tablespoon oil
> 500g/1lb coarsely minced chicken thigh meat
> ½ teaspoon five spice powder
> 2 tablespoons chopped coriander leaf
> 50g/2oz bamboo shoots or water chestnuts, chopped
> 300ml/½ pint chicken stock
> 8 slices fresh ginger
> 2 or more cloves garlic sliced

Rinse the cabbage leaves, remove any thick central spine and cut in half on the spine line. Lay around a large platter and microwave uncovered on High until steaming, bright green and beginning to soften, which will take 3 minutes or more. Cover with a tea towel to keep warm and pliable.

Use your hands lightly to mix together the chicken, five-spice, coriander, and bamboo or water chestnuts (or use a mixture of both). Put a portion into the bottom end of a cabbage leaf, roll once, turn in the sides and roll up quite tightly. Continue until all the leaves are stuffed; any extra chicken should be rolled into small balls. Arrange the rolls pointing inwards around a large shallow dish. Pinch each one in to a neat pointed shape, so the rolls are not touching each other. Pour on the stock, strew the ginger and garlic. Cover and cook on High for 5 minutes. Spoon the stock over the rolls, recover and cook another 10 minutes on PL5/Medium spooning over the stock one more time. Let them sit in the stock for 10 minutes if you can.

Serve in a bowl so you can share out the stock, removing the ginger pieces as you go.

Beetroot salsa

Not a chutney, not a pickle, but something like both of them – without the sauces. Its deep earthy colour is startling when served warm with hot or cold meats, and it makes a terrific and welcome change from pickles and relishes you know. Plus, it's another winning way to use up the crystallised ginger you always have left over from Christmas. Ginger can be confusing: the stuff I mean is covered in sugar and nicely chewy. Preserved ginger in syrup could be substituted.

Fills a 750g jar

500g/1lb evenly sized raw beetroot, small rather
   than large
3 tablespoons red wine vinegar
50g/2oz crystallised ginger, chopped
12 dried apricots, sliced
2 tablespoons currants
8 whole cloves
½ teaspoon cardamom seeds, lightly crushed
2 cloves garlic, sliced
1 generous teaspoon dried mint
2-4 tablespoons white sugar
1 teaspoon salt
Plenty of freshly ground black pepper

Peel and dice the raw beetroot. Combine with the vinegar, cover and cook on High for 5 minutes. Mix in all the remaining ingredients except the pepper, Cover and heat on High for 5 minutes. Add plenty of black pepper, stir well, and then serve as it is or let it cool covered. Better, of course, if made well in advance. Terrific slightly warmed with cold meats.

Two-cheese polenta

Tricky to describe, this. Because polenta is cornmeal, and that is a grain, polenta can be thought of as the basis of a main course, like rice or pasta but then, like vegetables it is also an accompaniment. That is what it is here, served soft and smooth rather than firm and grilled, as is more usual.

Even the modern fast-cooking polenta can be a problem in kitchens, as all polenta spits and burns terribly. But you are safe from burns when polenta is cooked in the microwave – and you won't get lumps. Guaranteed.

Serves 4 or more

175g/6oz instant polenta
1 litre/2 pints boiling water
2 teaspoons salt
4 tablespoons olive oil
4 tablespoons butter
85g/3oz Parmesan cheese, roughly diced
125g/5oz Dolcelatte cheese, cubed

Note: the metric version is not the usual alternative recipe, but an equivalent. The Parmesan is essential, but the Dolcelatte may be left out.

Put the polenta into a large deep glass casserole with a tight-fitting lid. Pour on the boiling water and then add the salt and the olive oil. Stir well and then put on the lid. Cook on a trivet on High for 4½ minutes or until well bubbling. Remove and stir thoroughly until the bubbling ceases. Cover again and allow to stand for at least 5 minutes, when it will thicken further.

Now is a good opportunity to prepare the cheese. The Dolcelatte should be chilled and firm and cut into cubes about 2cm/¾", and ideally be free of outside skin if you can manage that. If you like strong flavours use Gorgonzola instead.

Stir in the butter very well and then fold in the two cheeses lightly, so they do not break up too much.

Serve as a first course, just as it is with good bread, or as an accompaniment to almost anything, especially roasted and grilled meats, or roasted and grilled Mediterranean-style vegetables.

Double-rich horseradish potatoes

An unusual flavour combination which is winning, warming and gratifying. Particularly good served with roasted meats or with grilled seafood. This sort of dish normally takes up to 2 hours both to cook and absorb the cream.

Serves 4–6

   1kg/2lb, floury potatoes
   4-6 cloves garlic, finely chopped
   freshly grated nutmeg
   3 tablespoons creamed horseradish
   salt and pepper
   450ml/¾ pint double cream

This recipe is slightly different from that you saw in the series – and even better! Wash the potatoes but do not peel them: King Edwards are by far the best variety. Slice thinly, and then layer with the garlic, nutmeg, seasoning and creamed horseradish in a high sided casserole with a lid. Pour on just 150ml/¼ pint of the double cream and ensure it is evenly distributed. Cook covered on High for 8 minutes. Take off the lid and pour on the rest of the cream.

Now cook uncovered at a lower temperature (this is the difference from the original instructions) at PL5/ Medium for 20-30 minutes or until you are sure the potatoes are all tender. The cream will be bubbling and reducing and some of it may oil slightly, but this will disappear when you serve.

Let the mixture cool slightly and then chop and stir

to make a rough texture. Now taste and add a little more seasoning, horseradish or nutmeg to taste. Even better if allowed to cool before being reheated.

Parmesan pumpkin ring

A golden circle of pumpkin veined with a rugged thyme-fragranced mix of Parmesan, parsley, tomato and black olive.

Serves 6 or more

> 1 litre/1½ pints pumpkin purée (see method)
> 3 tablespoons olive oil
> Few drops Tabasco or other chilli sauce
> salt and pepper to taste
> 6 eggs
> 250g/8oz Parmesan or pecorino, coarsely
>   chopped
> 200g/8oz can chopped plum tomatoes, drained
> 2-4 cloves garlic, roughly chopped
> 50g/2oz flat leaf parsley, coarsely chopped
> 50g/2oz pitted black olives, roughly chopped
> 1 teaspoon fresh thyme leaves/scant teaspoon
>   dried

Begin with 1.5kg/3lbs or more of a really firm sweet pumpkin. The gourd shaped butternut is one of the best bets of all.

Cut the pumpkin roughly into small pieces, leaving the skin on. Put into large bowl, add a few tablespoons of water, cover and microwave until tender, 12–15 minutes according to type. Let it cool and then scrape off the flesh, mash or purée roughly and measure. Make up any shortfall with milk or cream.

Stir in the olive oil and then whisk the eggs and add them too: flavour to your taste with Tabasco, salt and pepper.

Lightly oil a large circular glass mould with olive oil,

perhaps lining the base with paper too. If you have no ring mould, use a 2-litre/4 pint flat-bottomed, high-sided glass baking dish and stand a heavy-bottomed glass in the middle. Mix together 150g/6oz only of the roughly chopped cheese, the drained tomatoes, the garlic, parsley, olives and thyme. Lightly season with black pepper but no salt. Ladle half the pumpkin mixture into the ring then add the cheese mixture evenly. Ladle on the remaining pumpkin mixture and then use a knife to gently swirl the mixture back and forth a couple of times.

Cook uncovered on a trivet on PL5/Medium for 25 minutes or until just set. Let it rest at least 10 minutes, uncovered, then ease the sides with a sharp knife and invert on to a platter. Sprinkle with the remaining Parmesan, perhaps mixed with more chopped parsley and olives too.

Serve in generous wedges, perhaps after filling the centre with a braised Mediterranean vegetable medley, or with something as simple as green peas. But do pour on a little more olive oil on and serve with lemon wedges.

White curry of potatoes, chickpeas and green peas

A lightly spiced vegetarian dish based on the culinary customs of Sri Lanka.

Serves 6 or more

750g/1½ lbs potatoes, peeled
400g can chickpeas, drained
250g/8oz frozen peas
2 tablespoons vegetable oil
1 or 2 cinnamon sticks
1 teaspoon coriander seed
6 cardamom pods, lightly crushed
¼ teaspoon turmeric
12 black peppercorns
1 or 2 green chillies, deseeded
2 or more cloves garlic, sliced
2 fresh limes
250g/8oz (approx) packet coconut cream
600ml/1 pint water
1-2 teaspoons salt

Mix the oil with the coriander, cardamom, turmeric, pepper, chillies and garlic. Microwave covered on High for 2 minutes or until the spices are lightly browned and smelling fragrantly. Turn into a large casserole with a tight-fitting lid. Cut the potatoes into large cubes, quarters or halves, about 5 cm/2" square and then turn in the spice mixture. Cover and microwave on High for 8 minutes. Whilst they are hot, squeeze on the juice of the limes, add the chickpeas and mix well. Replace the lid. May be prepared to this stage and kept refrigerated.

To continue, break up the coconut cream and put into a bowl with the water. Microwave on High for 2 minutes or until you can whisk it to a smooth cream. Pour over the potato mixture. Add the peas. Zest the skins of the limes and add together with a teaspoon of salt. Turn gently to mix without breaking the potatoes. Cover and microwave on High for 8 minutes or until thoroughly heated through. Let it stand 5 minutes or more before serving. Outstandingly good cold as an unusual buffet or barbecue dish.

Mediterranean patty pan squash

This recipe can also be used for chunks of pumpkin and squash or for generous rounds of courgette. Be sure to serve as soon as the basil leaves have been stirred in, to get the maximum effect of their peppery fragrance.

Serves 4–6

> 500g/1lb small patty pan squash
> 8 cloves garlic in their skin
> 50g/2oz sun dried tomatoes, thinly sliced
> 2 sprigs fresh thyme
> 6 tablespoons white wine
> extra virgin olive oil to taste
> handful of fresh basil leaves

Mix the garlic, sun-dried tomatoes, thyme and white wine into a small container, cover and cook on High for 4 minutes, which should give you tender garlic and nicely plumped tomato strips. Keep warm and covered. Meanwhile, cut the patty pan squash – ideally a mixture of yellow and green varieties – into quarters and cook covered (with no extra liquid) on High for 8-10 minutes, ensuring they do not lose their shape or bright colour. Whilst they are still hot, season lightly, and toss in enough good throaty olive oil to coat all of the pieces. Now toss in the garlic-tomato mixture and, finally, the basil leaves. Serve at once. This can also be terrific served cold, in which case use minimal olive oil, chill lightly, mix again, and only then pour on rather more oil.

If you are not using it elsewhere, freshly grated Parmesan cheese would be a delicious bonus.

Maharajah's gilded fruit pilau

A terrific centre piece for parties, buffets or any other special meal. If you want to go the whole way, ask a good local Indian restaurant if they can sell you some edible gold leaf to patch on the top.

Serves 6–8

6 tablespoons butter
6 whole cloves
6 cardamom pods, lightly crushed
1 teaspoon mustard seed
1 teaspoon cumin seed
1 teaspoon coriander seed, lightly crushed
¼ teaspoon or more saffron threads
1 cinnamon stick
2 teaspoons salt
350g/12oz basmati rice
500ml/18fl oz stock or water
750g/1½lb trimmed weight fresh fruit –
   peaches, plums, apples, pineapple, etc.
edible gold leaf (optional)

Put the butter and spices into a large casserole with a tight-fitting lid. Cook on High for 3 minutes. Stir in the salt and the rice until evenly coated. Pour on the stock or water, stir, cover and cook on High for 9 minutes.

The fruit should be in big generous pieces, no less than eighths for apples or peaches, for instance. Put these on top of the rice, cover again and cook on High for 6 minutes. Allow to rest for 3 minutes or more, then spoon out on to a large platter, mixing in the fruit without breaking it up.

Add edible gold leaf if you wish and serve with any sort of Indian meal.

A vegetable moussaka

*Moussaka doesn't have to include meat and can be made
with vegetables other than aubergines. The classic moussaka is topped with an egg-thickened cheese sauce, but here
our vegetarian moussaka is served with a quicker-to-make
cheese sauce, much more 90s.*

Serves 4–6

> 500g/1lb large aubergines
> 250g/8oz potatoes, thinly sliced
> 100g/4oz courgette, thinly sliced
> 200g/6oz yellow or red pepper, in large pieces
> 100g/4oz onion or leek, thinly sliced
> 2 cloves garlic, chopped
> 50g/2oz parsley, coarsely chopped
> 2 mint sprigs, chopped
> or ½ teaspoon dried oregano
> 200g can chopped plum tomatoes
> 200g can cannelini beans or chickpeas
> ½–1 teaspoon salt
> 4–6 tablespoons olive oil, or more
>
> 50g/2oz butter
> 40g/1½oz plain flour
> 600ml/1 pint milk
> 100g/4oz strong Cheddar cheese
> freshly grated nutmeg

Cut off the green end of the aubergine and then slice
quite thinly on an angle. Sprinkle both sides of each
piece lightly with salt and lay on a rack to drain for 20
or 30 minutes. Rinse and pat dry. Microwave on High
for 5 minutes, drain and sprinkle with olive oil. Microwave the slabs of red pepper on High for 5 minutes or
until tender

Choose a deep, round or oblong baking dish with at
least 1 litre/2 pints capacity. Line the bottom and sides

with aubergine slices, overlapping slightly as you go and leaving enough for a top layer.

Mix together the leek, garlic, parsley, mint or oregano, tomato and salt. Lightly crush the beans or chickpeas and mix into that. Then layer the vegetables: start with potato, add some courgettes, then potato: sprinkle each layer with olive oil plus a share of the prepared mixture. Put all the prepared pepper in a single middle layer. Make a final topping of aubergine slices and sprinkle that generously with olive oil. Press down well and cook uncovered on a trivet for 15 minutes on PL5/Medium or until the vegetables are really tender.

While this rests for a good 10 minutes before serving, melt the butter in a large jug, about 30 seconds on High, add the flour, mix and cook for another minute on High, being careful not to let it burn or brown. Whisk in the milk and cook on High for 3–5 minutes or until boiling and thickened, whisking at least once. Stir in the cheese and whisk. Flavour lightly with salt, pepper and nutmeg, and dilute with more milk if you like.

Cut the moussaka into even portions, serve on warm plates and pour the sauce around rather than over it, yes, that's right, like custard.

Black beans with greens and smoked tofu

Very much Southern in style, but replacing the more usual pork hock with smoked tofu. The wonderfully flavoured stock and the juices of the greens make this a real down-home flavour to be enjoyed with spoons, so serve in flat soup bowls with lots of good bread. If you like, make a thicker texture by mashing some of the beans half way through the heating.

Serves 4 or more

> 2 x 400g cans black beans
> 125g/4oz each onion, celery and green pepper
> 2–4 cloves garlic
> 2 tablespoons vegetable oil
> 300ml/½ pint vegetable stock
> 250g/8oz smoked tofu, cubed
> 1lb fresh spinach, beet or other greens

Drain the beans. Chop the onion, celery and green pepper evenly and finely, slice the garlic. Mix with the oil in a large glass bowl, cover and microwave on High for 5–7 minutes, or until the mixture is really soft.

Layer the beans and the smoked tofu on the mixture and then stir very gently so you do not break up the tofu. Cover and heat thoroughly, another 5 minutes or more. Let it sit for 5–10 minutes, covered, which will help develop the flavour more.

When ready to serve, rinse the greens and shake off the excess. Layer on top of the beans, cover and cook until just wilted, 3 to 5 minutes. Mix as you serve, and accompany with plenty of decent bread. Some would like a drop or two of chilli sauce with this, and you can add more stock to make the dish wetter and more soup like, too.

Vegetarian Boston baked beans

Of course baked beans are vegetarian you might say. Except real Boston beans always contained salt pork, but never featured tomato. Although not containing pork, this recipe is equally filling and gratifying and meat eaters can always add sausage, bacon or salt pork to their helping if they must. Make the traditional dark version with dark brown sugar and molasses, or go the lighter way and use maple syrup and light brown sugar; both are excellent with Boston Brown Bread made in minutes just before serving.

Serves 4 or more

> 2 x 400g cans cannelini or other white bean
> 250g/8oz onion, chopped (optional)
> 300ml/½ pint vegetable stock
> 2 tablespoons Worcestershire sauce
> 1 teaspoon mustard powder
> 4 tablespoons dark brown or light brown sugar
> 4 tablespoons molasses or maple syrup

If you have a well flavoured stock on hand you will not need the onion: if you have no stock use the onion and water: top the onion with a few tablespoons of butter and cook covered on High for up to 5 minutes. Then stir in the beans, the stock or water, and remaining ingredients. Otherwise just combine all the ingredients with stock. Cook covered on High for 10 minutes, remove, stir well. Cover and cook a further 30 minutes on PL5/Medium or until the liquid has reduced and some of the beans are breaking up. Extra stock or water can be added if the beans look dry. Taste and salt. Add more savouriness with Worcestershire sauce, or sweetness with the sugar if you want.

Much better if allowed to sit overnight before reheating.

Boston brown bread

This was classically steamed in closed containers, some-times old coffee tins. Then it was uncovered and put into the oven to crisp the top. What took an hour or more tradition-ally can be done in a tenth of the time by the microwave without losing any of the traditional flavour or effect. Orig-inally made with as many as three flours – wheat, cornmeal and rye for instance – it's just as authentic made with only wholemeal flour, or half white and half wholemeal. It's the molasses and the steaming which make this bread so spe-cial.

If your conventional oven is on, or you have a microwave which includes a conventional heat facility, you might like to crisp the crust, but I have never found it makes much difference. This is delicious anyway.

Serves 4–6

   350g/12oz wholemeal flour (or half and half)
   2 teaspoons baking powder
   1 level teaspoon salt
   150ml/5fl oz molasses or treacle
   450ml/¾ pint creamy milk

Mix together the dry ingredients. Whisk the molasses and milk together and stir to make a light dough. Put half the amount into a lightly oiled or buttered glass jug or other utensil with a 600ml/1 pint capacity. Keep the other half cool or the baking powder will begin to work.

Stand the container on a trivet, cover lightly with vented cling film and cook on PL5/Medium for 5–6 minutes. Remove from oven, uncover and stand for 5 minutes. Unmould and then regrease the cooking utensil and repeat with remaining batter. May be crisped. Pull apart to serve rather than trying to slice.

Curried peanuts

An unusual vegetarian dish to serve with rice and other vegetables, which can also be used as buffet or snack food or as a first course. If you can't easily buy peanuts which are raw but skinless, blanched almonds or cashew nuts do just as nicely, but cost more.

Serves 4 as a main course in an Asian-style meal

25g/1oz butter
1 tablespoon vegetable oil
100g/4oz onion, finely chopped
1 tablespoon fresh ginger, grated
2 teaspoons ground cumin
1 teaspoon ground turmeric
1 teaspoon garam masala
250ml/8floz hot vegetable stock or water
2 small red chillies, deseeded and chopped
350g/12oz peanuts, raw, skinless and unsalted
2 tablespoons fresh coriander, roughly choppped

Put the butter, oil and onion in a bowl big enough to take all the ingredients eventually and cook for 1 minute on High. Stir in the ginger, spices, chillies and peanuts. Cook on High for 3 minutes, stirring occasionally. The flavours should all have developed well and smell delicious. Cook on to deepen the flavour if you wish, being careful of burning. If you cannot easily buy chillies or don't know how hot the ones are that you buy, use Tabasco sauce instead, but with just as much care.

Now add the hot water or stock and cook on High for another 5 minutes, stirring a few times, by which time the nuts will have absorbed much of the liquid. Let it cool to tepid and then stir in the coriander.

As a snack or first course, serve with plenty of crisp very cold lettuce leaves, roll a spoonful of the peanut curry in a leaf and enjoy the contrast of textures and flavours.

Provençal spinach in a pesto-pasta crust

A surprising traditional mixture of spinach with currants and toasted pinenuts on a bed of Provence's equally traditional noodles, but this time flavoured with the pesto of Genoa, also based on pinenuts. A surprising first course, a special accompaniment or a main course for summer.

Serves 6–8

150g/6oz flat egg noodles (tagliatelle), dry
  weight
2 eggs
4 tablespoons pesto sauce
500g/1lb fresh baby spinach leaves, damp
50g/2oz pinenuts
25g/1oz currants
4 tablespoons olive oil
salt and pepper
a wedge of fresh Parmesan cheese

Cook the noodles in boiling salted water until just tender. Drain and let it steam dry. Meanwhile, whisk together the eggs and half the pesto sauce, and then toss the pasta in this mixture. Distribute evenly into a 22 cm/8½" diameter glass pie dish, looping a few of the pasta ends over the side to help keep everything in place. Press well and then cook uncovered on High for 3 minutes.

Brown the pinenuts by spreading them on a flat dish and cooking on High for 2 minutes, stir about and continue in 20-second bursts until they are evenly toasted.

The spinach should be well washed, but damp rather than wet. Cook covered on High for 3–4 minutes (depending on how well you have packed it and how wet it is), just enough to wilt it but to leave decent texture and crunch. Put the prepared pasta shell back into heat for just 1 minute on High. Working quickly, drain any excess moisture off the spinach. Season with salt and pepper and toss with the olive oil, currants and prepared pinenuts.

Spread the remaining pesto over the pasta shell. Tip in the spinach, piling it high and loose for the best effect. Use a vegetable peeler to make long curls of the Parmesan cheese, which should fall casually and unevenly over the top. Cut into large wedges to serve whilst still warm.

Cumin chickpeas in chilled lettuce leaves

The Chinese like to serve food like this, a big hot bowl of something succulent with crisp lettuce leaves. Rolling one in the other gives diners something to do and talk about, breaking the ice. An excellent idea for buffets too.

Serves 6 or more

2 x 400g cans chickpeas
4 tablespoons olive oil
1 tablespoon cumin seeds
4–6 tablespoons tomato purée
4 tablespoons chopped coriander or parsley
150g/6oz feta cheese, crumbled
crisp lettuce leaves, split lengthways if large

Mix the olive oil and cumin seeds in a container large enough to hold the chickpeas eventually. Heat on High for 3 or more minutes or until the cumin seeds have begun to colour and are smelling highly. Quickly stir in the tomato purée and then the chickpeas. Cover with a largish plate and heat through on High for 4–5 minutes and then add the chopped coriander or parsley and stir through. Tip on to the hot plate which has covered the bowl, pile high and then sprinkle with the feta cheese. Serve at once with a spoon for everyone. Show them how to put a dollop of hot chickpeas into a cold lettuce leaf, roll it up – and enjoy.

Baked yellow peppers with chunky chilli almonds

An excellent vegetarian main course and perfect buffet, bar-becue or picnic fare, too.

Serves 6

3 large yellow peppers
50g/2oz feta cheese, cubed
250g/8oz ricotta cheese
small carton thick natural yoghurt
4 tablespoons mint, chopped
zest of small lemon of half large lemon
15g/½ oz dry white bread crumbs
2 eggs
50g/2oz almond, roughly chopped
1–2 tablespoons chilli sauce

Cut the peppers in half from top to bottom, through the stalks if they are still attached. Remove excess membrane from inside and arrange cut side down. Microwave on High for 4 minutes. Turn over.

Mix the cheeses with the yoghurt, mint, lemon, crumbs and eggs and stuff into the pepper shells. Cook on a trivet on High for 8 minutes or until the mixture is nicely set. Best served warm rather than hot.

Mix the almonds with the chilli sauce (a Chinese chilli and garlic sauce is even better) – just enough to coat them well. Spread on a flat plate, push into a doughnut shape and microwave on High for 2 minutes or more, until the nuts begin to smell and the sauce has dried and caramelised a little. Scatter over the stuffed peppers.

White bean stew with a tequila salsa

A vegetarian meal out of cans and made in minutes. But frankly, even if you had the time to do it all the old fashioned way, the results would be no better. Like all such wet food, this is better if you can make it the day before and then reheat it to serve.

Serves 6–8 or more

2 x 400g cans cannelini beans
400g can chopped tomatoes
8–12 whole garlic cloves
4 sprigs fresh thyme
8 tablespoons rich olive oil
salt and pepper to taste

For the salsa
½ small red pepper
½ small yellow pepper
½ hot red chilli pepper
½ hot green chilli pepper
15g/½oz fresh coriander
15g/½oz flat leaf parsley
flesh of a small orange
flesh of a lime
1 heaped teaspoon chilli seasoning, hot or mild
2 tablespoons tequila

Mix all the ingredients for the stew together in a large container, cover and cook on High for 10–15 minutes or until the oil and tomatoes have boiled together to thicken slightly. You can get a thicker sauce for the beans by mashing up to a quarter of them and stirring well.

Put the salsa ingredients into a processor and pulse until evenly chopped but stop well before they are a purée or mush. Serve on to the top of the beans or in individual servings.

Roasted peanut-chilli and lime dipping sauce

Make this to serve with any plainly cooked or grilled meat, poultry or fish. Especially god as a better, brighter tasting sauce than satay for kebabs. May be used as a marinade or basting sauce too, but the sugar content means it will tend to burn if you lose your concentration.

Makes about 300ml/½ pint

85g/3oz raw, unsalted peanuts
150ml/¼ pint cider vinegar
100g/4oz caster or light brown sugar
2 teaspoons ginger, grated fresh
zest and juice of 2 limes,
1 small fresh red chilli pepper, deseeded and
  finely chopped
2 tablespoons very finely chopped lemon grass,
  bulb only
3 teaspoons of Thai fish sauce or light soy sauce
1 tablespoon fresh mint, chopped
1 tablespoon fresh coriander, chopped

Spread the peanuts in a ring shape on a flat plate and microwave on High for 3 minutes, stirring from time to time and rearranging into a ring. Cook on in 1-minute bursts until roasted as much as you like, but they should be at least lightly coloured. Process until finely chopped.

Microwave the limes for a minute or so to increase the juice yield. Combine the vinegar, sugar, ginger, lime zest and juice, chilli and lemon grass. Microwave on High for 3 minutes or until the sugar is dissolved, stirring occasionally. Stir in the peanuts and cook for another minute on High which thickens the sauce slightly. Then stir in the fish sauce and the herbs.

May be used hot or cold. A few chopped cloves of garlic may be added to the vinegar mixture, and more fresh herbs can be added just before serving to brighten the flavour further. Light soy sauce may be used instead of the fish sauce.

A modern fondue

The great party-dish of Switzerland – and of the rest of the world in the 60s and 70s – is enjoying a well deserved comeback. But instead of serving just chunks of white bread, pile the table with raw and roasted or grilled vegetables and all kinds of ethnic breads . . . and there are no flames or fumes at the table. You can use other cheeses, but nothing tastes quite like the real thing.

Serves 4 or more

> **200g/7oz Swiss Emmental, coarsely grated**
> **400g/14oz Swiss Gruyère, coarsely grated**
> **1 clove garlic**
> **300ml/½ pint white wine**
> **1 heaped teaspoon cornflour**
> **small glass kirsch or eau-de-vie**
> **white pepper, nutmeg**

Mix the two cheeses well and then rub a suitable bowl well with the cut clove of garlic. Ideally the bowl should be suited to going directly to the table. Add the wine to the bowl and microwave uncovered on High for 3–5 minutes, or until the wine is bubbling and close to boiling. Stir in the cheese and then microwave on High for 1 minute and stir again. Once the cheese has melted into a creamy mixture, mix the cornflour with the kirsch and then stir it in. Microwave on Medium/PL5 for 5 minutes. Give it a good stir and flavour with nutmeg and white pepper. If the fondue cools and starts to thicken before you have finished eating, reheat in 1-minute bursts on High – or put the fondue over the classic spirit burner.

Gingered kumquat and pecan relish

Serve straight away or keep to serve either warm or cold; other sharp-tasting citrus, cut small, may be used but will take longer to soften. For lamb, poultry and game.

Makes about 350g/12oz – 1 jar

250g/8oz fresh kumquats
50g/2oz glacé ginger chopped
1 cinnamon stick, halved
6 cloves
6 cardamom pods, lightly crushed
½ teaspoon coriander seeds
½ teaspoon black peppercorns
teaspoon salt
3 tablespoons muscavado sugar
3 tablespoons sherry vinegar
25g/1oz pecans, broken

Cut the kumquats in quarters lengthways and remove the pips as you go. Crush the coriander and peppercorns. Put the kumquats into a small container and mix in the ginger, spices and salt. Add 150mls/¼ pint water. Cover with a plate and cook on High for 10-12 minutes or until the skins are tender; the liquid should almost disappear. Stir in the salt, sugar and sherry vinegar.

Scatter the pecans over a large flat plate and microwave uncovered for 2 minutes, then push into a doughnut shape and continue in shorter bursts until nicely browned. Stir these in. Keeps well in a screw top jar, turned from time to time, in a cool place.

Fish and seafood

Warm avocado and prawns with a hot Thai vinaigrette

The world's favourite first course brought right up to date with a new presentation and a sparkling Asian flavour.

Serves 6

> 3 ripe, but firm avocados
> 350g/12oz cooked peeled prawns, defrosted
> 3 tablespoons vegetable oil
> 1 tablespoon cider vinegar
> 2 tablespoons lime juice
> 1 teaspoon prepared Thai Green Curry paste
> 1 tablespoon very finely chopped lemon grass
>   bulb
> 2 tablespoons basil leaves, finely julienned
> extra lime or lemon juice

Halve the avocados and remove the stones. As you do them, turn each half on its side and slice off the outer curve, ideally just cutting into the bottom of the pit from which the stone came. The main piece of avocado should now be about 2.5cm/1" thick and sit flat. Cut an even criss cross through the flesh to the skin of the oval-shaped pieces you have cut off. Paint all the exposed surfaces with lemon juice. Arrange the avocados around the edge of a large round plate, with the pointed edges inwards, with the small pieces on the large ones.

When ready to serve, first heat the avocados on High for 3 to 4 minutes, according to whether they are room temperature or not, by which time they will be hot but still firm. Remove. They will keep hot for quite some time. Meanwhile mix the sliced basil leaves into the prawns. Mix the oil, vinegar, lime juice, Green Curry Paste and lemon grass together in a jug and heat for 1 minute. Pour on to the prawns, mix, cover with a plate and heat on High for just 30 seconds.

Serve one piece of prepared avocado on to a warm plate. Spoon some prawns and their warm dressing sauce into the hole in the avocado, allowing some to tumble out on to the plate. Decorate with the incised smaller pieces. A large sprig of fresh basil makes a good final touch.

Stuffed sardines in manzanilla sherry

The clean saltiness of manzanilla, the driest of all sherries and aged by the Atlantic, will add an extra sense of the sea to the sardines. A terrific first course or snack on summer days. Frozen sardines are excellent value and often fresher and better than those you buy supposedly fresh.

Serves up to 6

12 fresh or frozen sardines
25g/1oz fresh white bread
25g/1 oz parsley
zest of 1 lemon
1 sachet of saffron powder
or a pinch of saffron threads
3 tablespoons olive oil
3 tablespoons lemon juice
6 tablespoons manzanilla sherry

The sardines should be scaled and gutted and the gills must be assiduously removed. Process the bread, parsley, lemon zest and saffron, perhaps adding a little garlic if you like. Stuff the sardines with this mixture and arrange head to tail in a shallow microwave-safe dish into which they just fit. Slash the top side of each sardine two or three times, and pour on the olive oil and lemon juice. These may be cooked covered or uncovered: the latter gives a drier texture, more like grilling. Either way, cook on High for 3 minutes only. Let sit for up to 5 minutes to even out the temperature and then pour on the sherry. Tip the dish back and forth to mix all the cooking juices with the sherry. Cool and lightly chill. Serve with good bread and more olive oil, of course.

Dim sum buns

The traditional flavour of this succulent Chinese snack re-lies on lard in the yeasted dough, but butter or other fat can be used. These can be quickly cooked in the microwave with-out further steam, but the effect is much greater when they come to table in a bamboo steamer.

To make 12 buns

    250g/8oz strong white bread flour, plus
    1 packet quick-mix yeast
    200ml/6 fl oz warm water
    2 teaspoons sugar
    2 heaped teaspoons lard, melted but cool
    12 squares rice paper or grease proof

Mix together the flour and yeast. Dissolve the sugar in the water and stir in the lard. Mix into the flour and knead well incorporating more flour as you do if the dough seems too soft, up to another couple of table-spoons. Leave to prove once under a damp cloth.

Each of the filling recipes is enough for 12 buns, but you might make less of each and serve a choice of fla-vours.

Prawn filling:

    100g/4oz raw prawns
    2 spring onions, chopped
    1 teaspoon chopped fresh ginger
    1 teaspoon light soy sauce
    few drops sesame oil

Process or chop to make an even paste: you might like to add some coriander leaf for colour and added fra-grance.

Chicken filling:

> **100g/4oz cooked chicken breast, chopped**
> **3 or 4 dried Chinese mushrooms**
> **Shao-Hsing rice wine or dry sherry**
> **4-6 water chestnuts (canned)**
> **1 tablespoon chopped coriander leaf**
> **1 teaspoon light soy sauce**
> **few drops sesame oil**

Remove and discard the stalk of the mushrooms and then soak the caps in water for 20 minutes. Drain and simmer for 5 minutes or until soft in a little rice wine or sherry. Put all the ingredients into a processor and blend until even.

To make the buns: roll the dough into a sausage shape and cut into 12 even pieces. Flatten each to about 10cm/4″ in diameter, put a generous teaspoon of filling in the centre of each and then draw up the sides with little pinches to end up looking rather like a dolly bag. It is easier to get a nice shape then to turn each over, to give a round bun shape. Put on to the prepared paper shapes. Cover with a damp cloth allowing space for each to expand and double in size – about 30 minutes. Now wet the bamboo steamer well.

When ready to serve, stand the buns directly on the bamboo slats. Boil some water, pour some into a shallow suitable bowl, stand the steamer on that and cook on High for about 2 minutes for 3 buns.

Note: If you do not have a bamboo steamer, cook the buns directly on your trivet – 6 should take between about 90 seconds and 2 minutes, but you will have to check as you go.

Porée of mixed fillets

This is a classic dish of the Charentes, the area which makes cognac, and where leeks are the very platform of good cookery. It takes some time to prepare the fish fillets, but the results are wondrous. A very elegant first course or light main course.

Serves 4

4 pink trout fillets, skinned
4 plaice fillets, skinned
4 red mullet fillets, skin on
2 tablespoons cognac
4 tablespoons fruity or sweet white wine
350g/12oz leeks, trimmed weight and of similar
   diameter
50g/2oz butter
small carton double cream

Inevitably, the trout fillets are likely to be bigger than the plaice ones and red mullet are notoriously different in size. But try for as even an effect as possible as this means more consistent cooking. For a first course you might like to choose small trout and mullet, which means the plaice fillets can each be only half the width of the fish. The mullet must keep its skin but have its bones removed: other fish fillets should be scaled and the remaining bones removed; eyebrow tweezers work well.

Mix together the cognac and half the white wine, and then bathe all the fillets in this mixture (Note: Pineau de Charentes, a mixture of brandy and grape juice may be substituted for the cognac and wine mixture). Now roll up the fish fillets always starting at the tail end. The trout and the plaice must be rolled with the skin side in, or they will unroll during cooking. The mullet should be rolled with the skin out. Pour on any more of the mixture and marinate for an hour or so.

Meanwhile, cut four equal lengths of leek, about 5cms/2" long. Put into a small covered bowl with the remaining two tablespoons of wine or Pineau. Slice the remaining leeks very finely and put them into another small covered bowl with the butter. Put these bowls into the microwave and cook for 2 minutes on High.

The big pieces should be tender: the small ones wilted but still a good colour.

To cook, arrange the buttered leeks around the outside edge of a round casserole dish which will hold the fish fillets and the leeks side by side around its circumference. Arrange the fish and the barrels of leek in a pretty, repeating pattern. Pour over any remaining marinade or buttery liquid. Cover and cook on a trivet for 4½ minutes on High.

Immediately add the cream to the centre, cover and allow stand for 5 minutes. Serve the fish and leek barrels on warm plates. Mix together the bed of sliced leeks with the cream and juices. Serve those leeks in a pile and pour the creamy liquid around, not over, the fish.

Vodka-dill prawns

Create your own version of this delicious and attractive dish by using a flavoured vodka: lemon or buffalo grass perhaps.

Serves 2–4

> 250g/8oz frozen raw tiger prawns, heads off,
>   shells on
> 6 tablespoons vodka
> 15g/½oz fresh dill
> 1 tablespoon butter
> 6 peppercorns
> 1 clove garlic, crushed

Reserve about a tenth of the dill, Put the rest into a microwave-safe jug and add the vodka, butter, peppercorns and garlic. Seal well with cling film (do not pierce or the alcohol will escape). Microwave on High for 1 minute and set to one side without disturbing the cling film.

Lay each prawn on its side and cut through the shell and flesh, leaving only the tail intact. Open out and press the tail hard so each prawn lies flat. Arrange them with their tails pointing inwards around the edge of a large plate.

Microwave the prawns uncovered (or covered for a softer texture) on High for 1½ minutes. Reheat the vodka mixture for 30 seconds on High. Chop the reserved dill and sprinkle over the prawns together with some freshly ground black pepper and a little salt. Strain the warm buttered vodka over the prawns and serve at once.

Warm tequila-soused goujons with a green salsa

Deep sea dory from New Zealand is especially good for this, but fillets of lemon sole or of orange roughy work too, keeping their shape and elasticity well.

Serves 2 as a main course, 4 as a first course

> **500g/1lb shallow, firm white fish fillets**
> **4 tablespoons tequila**
> **1 fresh lime**
> **1 teaspoon chili seasoning (not chilli or cayenne)**
> **1 seedless orange**
> **1 small avocado**
> **½ red pepper**
> **½ yellow pepper**
> **15g/½oz fresh coriander**
> **15g/½ oz fresh parsley**
> **½ teaspoon salt**
> **lime wedges and hot tortilla chips to serve**

Cut each fillet into three or four even strips lengthways, and cut each of those in half. Put into a flat microwave-safe dish and cover with the tequila, and the zest and juice of the lime. Add the chili seasoning and turn to cover evenly. Let it marinate for 1 hour at room temperature, 4 hours in a refrigerator (let it return to room temperature before proceeding).

Make the salsa. Cut the peel off the orange leaving no white behind. Cut each segment free by cutting between the membrane. Halve the avocado and remove the flesh in big scoops. Chop the peppers roughly. Now mix together with the coriander and parsley and chop by hand to an even texture. Or put all into a processor and work lightly – don't make a mush. Fold in salt to taste.

When ready to serve, cook the fish on High for 2 minutes. Rearrange the pieces, cook another minute and then allow it rest for 5 minutes. To serve, pile the warm deep sea dory pieces high in the centre of a plate. Spoon the salsa over the top. Serve at once with lime wedges and hot tortilla chips.

Shandong prawns

China's northeastern Shandong province provided most of the talented chefs for the Imperial kitchens. There they still create and experiment and I found them deep into the discovery of the pleasures of butter, especially with seafood.

Srves 2–6 as a first course

> 250g/8oz whole, raw prawns, biggest possible
> 40g/1 ½oz butter
> 2 tablespoons fresh coriander, chopped
> pinch five spice powder
> small clove garlic
> salt

The prawns look more impressive if you keep the heads, feelers and legs attached. Make a cut in the space where the head shell overlaps the body shell. Stop before you cut the prawn in half. Make another transverse cut like this just in front of the tail. Lay the prawn on its side and cut along the back to join the previous cuts, making an exaggerated 'I'. Remove the intestinal tract and rinse well.

Mix the ingredients for the butter and stuff into the cavities, including between the shell and the flesh. Put a half lime or lemon (emptied) in the centre of a large plate and attach the prawns to this with a toothpick, so all their heads are gathered together and the stuffed tails make spokes around the plate.

Cook uncovered on High for 2 minutes. A little Chinese or balsamic vinegar may be sprinkled as you serve.

Fish in banana leaves

If you cannot get banana leaves, non-stick baking parchment or grease proof paper do nicely, but will not give the extra fragrance.

Serves 4

4 thick fish steaks or cutlets, about 150g/6oz each
1 large lemon
50g/2oz onion
2.5cm/1" fresh ginger
2 green chillies, deseeded
50g/2oz fresh coriander, including stalks and roots
1 teaspoon ground cumin
50g/2oz desiccated coconut
1 tablespoon vegetable oil
1 or 2 teaspoons garam masala
4 banana leaves or baking paper

Make a flavouring masala by zesting the lemon into a large bowl, which will also collect the lemon oil. Peel away the remaining white, then cut out each segment of lemon flesh between the membranes. Stir the lemon and zest together to collect the lemon oil and put into a processor with the onion, ginger, chillies, cumin, coconut and oil. Make a paste of them and then cook covered on High for 1 minute. Whilst hot, stir in the garam masala, which should be fragrant, not hot.

Prepare four oiled pieces of banana leaf or baking paper each big enough to wrap one of the fish steaks. Sit each piece of fish on a bed of paste and smear the top with more. Seal, leaving some space on top – use toothpicks for the banana leaves. Arrange evenly around the edge of a flat plate, and leave for an hour or so to develop the flavours. Microwave on High for 5 minutes, stand for 2 minutes and then serve. Also good served cold.

Simple salmon steaks

These recipes are a good guide to cooking other types of fish. If the pieces are thinner they will cook faster, if thicker, slower.

Steaks, solid flesh cut from one side or a fillet of salmon are a better choice than cutlets cut across the central portion, as they are more evenly shaped and thus cook at the same rate.

Microwave poaching means the fish is accompanied by a little liquid and cooked covered. For 2 × 150g/6oz salmon steaks: put the steaks into a small flat dish and pour on 4–6 tablespoons of a fruity or medium sweet white wine. Dot with butter, sprinkle with parsley, cover and cook on High for 2½ minutes. Allow to sit for a few minutes, still covered.

Microwave baking means the fish is cooked uncovered with oil or butter and no other liquid. For 2 × 150g/6oz fillets, evenly shaped and sized: top with a tablespoon or so of chopped tomato, some chopped black olive, a little garlic and some parsley. Drizzle on some olive oil. As there is less liquid the fish will cook more quickly – 2 minutes on High. Allow it to rest before enjoying.

Pineapple and prawn curry

The finely balanced acidity and sweetness of pineapple is always good with seafood, here made even better by the richness of coconut cream. Leeks, too, are kinder than onions. Choose an Indian curry paste and the combination with lemon grass gives a Sri Lankan note; use green Thai curry paste and enjoy the popular flavours of that cuisine.

Serves 2–4

1 small or medium pineapple with top
1 tablespoon vegetable oil
200g/6oz leeks, finely sliced
1 tablespoon lemon grass, very finely sliced
1 tablespoon curry paste (to taste)
1 small cinnamon stick
1 teaspoon black peppercorns, crushed
1 tablespoon cornflour
400ml can coconut cream
250g/8oz cooked shelled prawns

Cut the pineapple in half lengthways. Cut down either side of the central woody core almost to the skin, taking care not to pierce it. Then cut from the core to the outer skin in slices about 2.5cm/1" wide, again going down to the skin but not piercing it. Cut out the shapes, discarding the tough pieces of core. Cut the flesh into squares. Turn the excavated cases over to drain, but keep the juice.

Put the oil, leeks, lemon grass, curry paste, cinnamon and crushed peppercorns into a bowl, stir well and cook on High for 3 minutes. Add the pineapple pieces and all the juice you collected, stir in and cook for another 3 minutes.

Mix the cornflour with a little water and stir into the coconut milk or cream. Mix evenly into the pineapple mixture. Cook uncovered on Medium for 3–5 minutes or until the mixture thickens and is piping hot.

Now add the prawns – you can double the amount – and heat through, still on Medium for another 3–5 minutes, or until the prawns are heated through. Stir gently.

Pile the hot mixture into the drained pineapple shells, garnish with lime wedges and coriander sprigs.

Riviera fish stew

All the best flavours of the French Riviera, and made with the same technique used for the bouillabaisses created by the fishermen of Marseilles – that is to marinate the fish long and well before cooking it quickly.

Serves 4

1kg/2lb boneless fish, see method
8 tablespoons olive oil
150ml/¼ pint fruity or medium sweet white wine
1 sachet saffron powder
or a generous pinch saffron threads
3 sprigs thyme
125g/4oz fennel, finely chopped
zest of half a large sweet orange
50g/2oz small pitted black olives
2 teaspoons Pernod, or to taste
4 tablespoons mayonnaise
4 garlic cloves, finely chopped
250g/8oz tomato, chopped
olive oil, parsley to serve

You could use just cod, but I chose a mixture of fish, which is more usual in this style of dish even though most are hard to get without bones. My mixture was 500g/1lb of cod, 250g/8oz conger eel and 250g/8oz prepared squid tubes, each about 15cm/6" long. The fish should be in chunks about 2.5cm/1", and to achieve an equal density with the squid, we simply cut each in half diagonally.

Mix together the olive oil, white wine, saffron, thyme, fennel, orange zest, olives and Pernod. Pour over the fish, and turn to ensure it is coated completely. Let it sit at room temperature for at least an hour, 4 hours in the refrigerator. Taste a little of the marinade and add more Pernod if you wish, but with restraint. Mix together the mayonnaise and garlic, cover and store at room temperature to develop maximum potency.

Arrange the fish in a single layer in a suitable casserole, cover and cook on a trivet for 4 minutes on High, then leave to sit for 5 minutes or so.

Top each serving with a dollop of the garlic mayonnaise and some parsley, scatter with chopped tomato, and then drizzle everything with very good olive oil. Serve with an olive oil mash, with or without more garlic.

Note: if you have or can make some genuine aioli, use this rather than the mixture of garlic and mayonnaise.

Shanghaied mackerel with a caramel-soy ginger sauce

Matchsticks of ginger are cooked in a caramel, which is then diluted with soy sauce to make the sort of rich, dark sauce so loved by the Shanghainese. Oily trevalli fillets, small fat snapper or just 2 small grey mullet all work just as well.

4 x mackerel 250g/8oz each, cleaned weight
½ teaspoon five-spice powder
50g/2oz caster sugar
25g/1oz fresh ginger root
8 tablespoons water
4 tablespoons dark soy sauce
1 teaspoon red wine or sherry vinegar (optional)

Choose fish which are roughly the same size. Cut a deep criss-cross pattern on the top of each and lightly rub in the five spice powder evenly.

Put the sugar and 4 tablespoons only of the water into a small microwave-safe glass bowl. Peel the ginger and cut into matchsticks. Add to the bowl. Microwave on High for 4 minutes or until the mixture is a rich dark brown – a pale colour is useless. Before it starts smoking and burning, add the remaining water, mixed with the soy sauce. Swirl the mixture, but do not stir with anything. Microwave for a further 30 seconds, swirl again and cover.

Arrange the mackerel on a large plate, like wheel spokes, with their tails to the centre. Cover lightly and cook on High for 3 minutes; leave to stand for a further 3–5 minutes whilst you complete the other cooking. Serve on to warm plates. Taste the sauce and add a little vinegar if you would like to further enhance the sweet-hot effect: quickly reheat and pour over the fillets, making an even distribution of the ginger pieces.

Snapper with a thyme-scented olive oil and an artichoke mash

A rugged mash made with olive oil is top of the culinary pops. Here the Mediterranean influence goes further with olives, capers, artichokes and a herb-scented oil for a sauce.

Serves 4

4 x 150g/6oz fillets New Zealand snapper (or cod)
150ml/¼ pint olive oil
10 or 12 sprigs fresh thyme or marjoram
2 cloves garlic
1kg/2lb potatoes, peeled, quartered
oil for mashing
16 black olives, pitted, roughly chopped
2 teaspoons capers
1 teaspoon fresh thyme or marjoram leaves
400g can artichoke hearts in brine

Put the first amount of oil into a microwave-safe jug or bowl with the thyme and garlic. Cover and microwave on High for 2½ minutes. Let it stand 30 minutes or longer if you can, still covered.

Put the potatoes into a large bowl, with no extra liquid, cover and microwave on High for 12 minutes. Allow to stand for a few minutes then uncover and mash roughly with olive oil, 3–4 tablespoons should do. Salt to taste. Roughly chop all but one of the drained artichokes and stir into the mash. Cover and keep warm.

Arrange the fish pieces on a large plate which will fit into the microwave. Mix together the chopped olives, capers, thyme leaves and remaining artichoke heart, roughly chopped. Scatter evenly on the fillets. Cover and microwave on High for 4 minutes or longer according to thickness: cook only until just set, then leave covered for a few minutes. Reheat the mash and serve the fillets with their toppings. Give the scented oil a short burst in the microwave and then strain over the fillets.

Couscous-stuffed squid on braised fennel

A recipe for when you have the time to muck about in the kitchen. And well worth the bit of a fiddle it can be.

Serves 6 as a first course, 2 or more as a main course

6 whole squid, about 150mm/6" body length each
500g/1lb fennel bulb plus green fronds
150ml/¼ pint medium white wine or light stock
3 lemons
3 tablespoons butter
3 tablespoons olive oil
85g/3oz couscous
3 tablespoons butter
4 sun-dried tomato halves, finely sliced

Cut off the tentacles, pull out the mouths and cut them off. Take hold of the quill's end pull firmly and remove. Pull back one of the upper fins and remove that, the other fin and the remainder of the outer membrane, giving you clean, white tubes: you can buy prepared tubes, but then you do not have squid pieces to put into the filling. Peel the fins and chop them roughly with the tentacles.

Cut off the green fronds of the fennel and reserve. Cut the fennel into thin slices from top to bottom across each bulb. Lay it around the base of a flat-bottomed circular dish. Microwave the lemons for 2 minutes on High. Juice two of them and put that into the fennel. Add the stock, 2 tablespoons of the olive oil and dot around 2 tablespoons of the butter.

Cover and cook on High for 15–20 minutes or until the fennel is really tender. This can be done well in advance.

Put the juice of the remaining lemon into a measuring jug and make the quantity up to 100ml/4 fl oz with water. Add the remaining olive oil and butter and then stir in the couscous. Cover and cook on High for 2 minutes. Let it sit for a few minutes then stir in the chopped fennel frond and chopped squid pieces.

Make a cut about 15mm/½" or so in the open end of each squid. Hold by one of the corners you have created and use a teaspoon to stuff with the couscous mixture. Squeeze it down gently, like milking a cow. At some stage, change to hold the squid like an ice cream cone, which makes it easier to push in the final stuffing. When ready to serve, reheat the fennel, then layer the squid on top, with their pointed ends towards the centre. Cover with a plate or cling film, and microwave on High for 3 minutes only. Let it rest for a few minutes. Cut each squid on an angle into five or six pieces. Arrange on the fennel, and pour over some juices.

Creole prawns

Classic Southern flavourings for a favourite ingredient. The sauce of this recipe will happily take up to 500g/1lb of prawns for a substantial supper dish, but half that amount is ideal for something lighter or a first course.

Serves 2–4, or perhaps 6 as a first course

250g–500g/8oz–1lb large cooked prawns
100g/4oz each, onion, celery, green pepper,
   finely and evenly chopped
2 or more cloves garlic, sliced
50g/2oz butter
400g can chopped plum tomatoes
1 heaped teaspoon sweet paprika
4–6 drops Tabasco sauce
or
1 fresh chilli pepper, chopped
2 generous tablespoons parsley, roughly chopped

In a large microwave-safe container, stir together the onion, celery, green pepper, garlic and butter. Cover and cook on High for 5 minutes or more depending on how finely chopped they are. The mixture should not colour or brown. Stir in the tomatoes, paprika, Tabasco or fresh chilli pepper. Cover and cook for 4 minutes on High. Stir well, and cook a little more if you think it should be hotter. Stir in the prawns: if they are refrigerated, heat for 2 minutes, but if at room temperature 1 minute will be enough or they will toughen. Stir in the parsley.

Serve with buttered plain rice and garnish with more parsley.

Stir fry of prawns, scallops and mangetout

The best looking colours and textures, cooked without the

clatter and smoke of a wok. Note that coating the fish with cornflour, traditionally called velveting, is not necessary, and that clearer, cleaner flavours and colours result from leaving it off the food. Up to you. . .

Serves 4 or more

> 6 large scallops with orange corals, or
>   equivalent smaller scallops
> 12 large raw prawns, shelled
> 100g/4oz mangetout
> 1 teaspoon cornflour
> 2 tablespoons Shao-Hsing rice wine or medium
>   sherry
> 1 teaspoon sesame oil
> ½ teaspoon salt
> 2 tablespoons vegetable oil
> 6 thin slices ginger, cut into matchsticks
> 3 spring onions, whites only, thinly sliced
> scattering of sesame seeds

Separate the scallops from their corals, remove the tough white muscle from the main flesh and discard. Slice each scallop across into 2 or 3 even slices. Dry these, the corals and the prawns. Put the scallop slices into a bowl, the corals and prawns into another. Sprinkle evenly with the cornflour (if using). Mix 1 tablespoon of the wine, the salt, the sesame oil and a teaspoon of the vegetable oil. Stir evenly into both bowls.

Trim the mangetout, put them into a bowl with a few tablespoons of water and cook on High for 1 minute, drain and reserve. Put the remaining vegetable oil, ginger and spring onions into a dish, cover and cook on High for 1 minute. Add the scallop slices, cook on High for 1 minute then tip on to a warm dish. Now cook the corals and prawns for 1 minute on High. Stir in the remaining wine, carefully mix in the scallops and mangetout and heat through for 40 seconds. Sprinkle with chopped coriander and serve.

Dill salmon and ruffled cucumber salad *en papilotte*

Scandinavian in inspiration. Salmon with a high-piled hot salad of cucumber, served in parchment. Very dinner party.

Serves 4

4 boneless cuts of salmon, 100g/4oz each
500g/1lb cucumber, trimmed but not peeled
1 tablespoon salt
4 tablespoons sherry or white wine vinegar
4 tablespoons white wine
1 tablespoon or more white sugar
25g/1oz fresh dill fronds
4 circles grease proof paper, 25cm/10" diameter

Make the salad in advance. Slice the cucumber paper thin, using a processor ideally. Toss in the salt and leave to drain in an oval lipped dish: tip up one end to assist the drainage and press the slices from time to time for about an hour. Give a final squeeze. Mix together the vinegar, wine and sugar and mix lightly through the cucumber, which encourages the ruffled look. Leave at room temperature for a couple of hours.

Lightly butter each piece of grease proof, ensuring the circumference is covered. Put a couple of fronds of fresh dill on the left of each piece of paper and put salmon on each (skin side down if you are using tail pieces). Salt and pepper the salmon, cover with the remaining dill and then arrange the cucumber on top, keeping it high and light and ruffled looking. Sprinkle on a few teaspoons of the marinade.

Fold and seal the paper tightly. Put evenly around a large flat plate with the thickest parts of the fish to the outside. Microwave on High for 3½ minutes.

Slide one on to each plate, garnish with extra dill. Open at table, and pass the remaining marinade as a sauce, perhaps slightly warmed.

Poultry and meat

Poached chicken breasts

Individual chicken breasts, boneless and skinless are an absolute standby of the modern kitchen. Microwave-poached in their own juices or with a little wine or stock, they are the basis of hundreds of meals and thousands of snacks.

For 2 breasts

2 boneless, skinless, individual chicken breasts
lemon, orange or lime zest
2 tablespoons white wine, vermouth, sherry or
  stock
small Boursin cheese

Chicken breasts must be cooked gently and have their outer membrane cut or pricked, or they might burst here and there. Most problems are avoided if you cut a shallow criss-cross in the top of each breast. Put the breasts in a shallow dish and grate lemon, orange or lime zest directly on to each, as much or as little as you like. Sprinkle with your chosen liquid and then cover with a plate or with cling film. Cook on a trivet at PL7/Medium High or lower for 4–5 minutes: they are done when there is only the slightest pink patch underneath, which will finish cooking when you stand them for 3–4 minutes, covered. Remove the breasts to a warm plate, and whisk half the Boursin cheese into the cooking liquid in the warm cooking dish. Then whisk in more to make a thicker sauce, according to your preference. One small Boursin will make a sauce for up to 4 breasts.

Slice the breasts on a shallow angle and pour the sauce around them. A little more freshly grated zest is always a good thing.

Note: Four individual breasts will take about 6–8 minutes. Add to cooking time if the breasts are direct from the refrigerator.

Other serving suggestions

Chicken breasts are much more adaptable and look better too, if they are pulled into long, generous strands, hot, warm or cold. And then you might make:

Chicken-filled baked potatoes
Steam jacket potatoes in the microwave and then crisp the skin in a conventional cooker. Sit upright on a warm plate and cut almost to the bottom, three or four times. Stuff chicken strands into the cuts, with plenty of salt and pepper as you go: add olive oil, warmed mayonnaise (just a few seconds in the microwave) or soured cream; plus roasted or grilled vegetables, and a modest sprinkle of coarsely chopped or flaked Parmesan cheese. Chilled salad in hot potatoes is also good, particularly watercress or rocket.

Chicken filo sandwiches
Squares of filo pastry painted with garlic butter or flavoured olive oil cook in a conventional oven in just a few minutes. For each person prepare 2 × 10–15cm/4" x 6" squares, each of at least four and up to six layers of filo pastry, each painted with melted butter of with olive oil. Half of them should have a criss-cross cut through the top layer of pastry, and these will be your top pieces. Bake for 5–8 minutes in a conventional cooker until golden brown and crisp all through. Keep warm, or make in advance and reheat gently.

Slice or strand the chicken. Invert one square of pastry and pile on to that some lightly dressed salad of interesting leaves, or some hot microwaved leaf spinach, roasted vegetables and sun dried tomatoes, sliced cheeses etc. Add the chicken, some more salad, and so on. Bathe with a little sauce or olive oil as you go if you like, top with the piece of pastry you have decorated.

New wave sandwiches
Lightly warm thin lavash or pitta bread, or split and toast focaccia. Fill the lavash with chicken and salad or

roasted and grilled vegetables and roll, then slice at an angle into smaller pieces. With the pitta simply split in half and stuff. Pile one half of each focaccia piece with chicken and fillings, top with the other half, squash and serve.

Stuffed chicken breasts

A highly-flavoured, moist stuffing makes a chicken breast into a much more substantial meal. Almost anything can be used, and the preparation technique is simple.

Essentially you begin by butterflying each breast. Turn an individual boneless and skinless chicken breast over so it lies with the original skin side on the board. Facing you on one side you will see a long fillet which can easily be pulled away – don't! Instead put the tip of a very sharp pointed knife into the flesh below it, as parallel to the board as possible and cut a pocket out towards the outer edge, taking care not to pierce that edge and taking it as far as you can towards the upper and lower points of the breast shape.

The side opposite the long fillet is much thinner: cut another pocket with the knife at the same angle, again from top to bottom. You should now be able to turn the top side of the pockets outwards to give a much bigger shape. This is what gets stuffed, smeared or flavoured, as you prefer.

Suggested fillings

Crab-meat, lime zest, finely chopped lemon grass and a sprinkle of Tabasco.

Hummous, chopped black olives, sprinkle of oregano, lemon juice or garlic.

Peppery watercress leaves and crumbled feta cheese.

A generous smear of black olive paste, slabs of roasted or canned red pepper, slices of fresh buffalo-milk mozzarella.

And a real surprise, Crusader's Chicken: grate orange zest directly on to the opened surface, sprinkle with nutmeg and cinnamon, spread with a top quality Christmas mincemeat and sprinkle with chopped toasted nuts. Very Middle Eastern and Jerusalem and an amazing talking point at a festive buffet

Now, roll the sides back again to cover your filling. Turn the breast back, right side up, and tuck the top and bottom under to ensure everything stays in place – you can use a long cocktail stick or two to be sure. Lightly score the top in a criss-cross pattern, being certain not to cut through to your filling. Put into a suitable shallow container, add a few spoonfuls of wine, stock or water, cover with cling film or a plate and microwave on PL5/Medium for 3½ minutes depending on the stuffing. Two breasts will take 3–6 minutes, according to size and stuffing. Let them sit for 3–4 minutes and then slice on an angle and serve.

Chinese chilli chicken

Marinading in advance increases the flavour tremendously, but the world won't end if you make, cook and enjoy the dish all at once. Excellent served in cold slices for buffets, picnics or with a salad.

Serves 4

  4 single chicken breast fillets, skinned
  2 garlic cloves, finely chopped
  1 teaspoon grated fresh ginger
  2 tablespoons Hoisin sauce
  2 tablespoons light soy sauce
  1 tablespoon sweet chilli sauce
  ¼ teaspoon five spice powder
  fresh coriander, chopped

Lightly slash the chicken breasts. Mix them together with all the ingredients except the coriander. Marinate at least an hour at room temperature or 4 hours refrigerated.

Arrange the breasts in a star shape around a plate with the pointed end facing inwards. Cover with another plate and cook on Medium-High for 4 minutes. Carefully uncover, turn each piece over and cook for another 4 minutes on Medium-High. Quickly pour the marinade into a jug and then recover the breasts and let stand. Heat the marinade for 3 minutes on High or until it has thickened somewhat. Serve the breasts sliced diagonally, spoon over the hot sauce and strew with the coriander.

Some roast almonds make an excellent extra garnish.

Chicken pasta with walnuts and dolcelatte

Serves 2

> **1 individual, boneless, skinless chicken breast**
> **2 teaspoons or more balsamic vinegar**
> **150g/6oz (dry weight) rigatoni or penne**
> **50g/2oz walnuts, chopped**
> **100g/4oz broccoli florets, absolute green tops only**
> **75g/3oz soft blue cheese (i.e. Castello), diced**

Score the chicken breast, sprinkle with balsamic vinegar – the better the quality, the less you'll use. Let it sit for an hour or so if you can.

Cook the pasta in plenty of well-salted boiling water. Meanwhile, microwave the chicken on PL7/Medium High for about 2 minutes. Leave covered. Arrange the walnuts in a ring on a flat plate and microwave on High for about 2 minutes, stirring once.

Once the pasta is cooked, drain and let steam for a few minutes. First, pull the chicken into long thick strands, and then cook the broccoli which should be only the final few millimetres of the florets – put them into a small bowl, sprinkle with water and cook 1½ minutes on High. Toss the pasta in just a few tablespoons of olive oil, and then add the chicken, walnuts, broccoli and cheese. Toss lightly and carefully, and then serve. Some sliced sun-dried tomato is terrific in this; predictable I know, but what isn't that is so good?

Mediterranean chicken in baked dough

This is based on Chinese beggar's chicken, a stuffed chicken steamed in clay. But once you get the idea this recipe can be adapted to any style of cuisine you like: use an Indian stuffing, something Creole or something Caribbean. It will always be a stunning dish to serve.

Serves 4–6

750g/1½lb strong white bread flour
600ml/1 pint water
1.5kg/3lb roasting chicken
1 small red pepper, finely sliced
2 cloves garlic, crushed
25g/1oz pine kernels
25g/1oz black olives, sliced
2–3 tablespoons pesto sauce
6–8 vine leaves

Mix together the water and flour to make a soft but firm dough. You are not going to eat it so, although it should be kneaded a little to encourage elasticity, it does not require a lot of attention. Oil the surface lightly and cover with a damp cloth.

Remove the shanks of the legs and the parson's nose of the chicken. Lift the skin over the breast and slide in your hands also to lift the skin over the top of the legs.

Cook the red peppers uncovered on High for 2 or 3 minutes until they are nicely tender. Sprinkle the pine kernels on a flat plate and cook on High for 2 minutes or until they are lightly browned, stirring from time to time. Mix together the pepper, garlic, pine kernels, black olives and pesto sauce and spoon the mixture evenly between the skin and breast of the chicken, ensuring some gets on to the top of the legs.

Roll out the dough and cover with the vine leaves which must be well soaked according to instructions. Put them shiny side down. Perhaps put a few extra leaves over the chicken breast, shiny side up.

Put the chicken on to the prepared dough and pull up the sides. Fold them together and make a good seal everywhere. Slash lightly without cutting through the dough. A little oil or butter rubbed into the dough would give a browner finish. Cook on High for 30 minutes and then leave to rest for 15 to 20 minutes.

To serve cut all around with a sharp knife about two-thirds down and remove the top. If you make some more of the stuffing mixture, it's a bright and delicious accompaniment.

Chicken and cashews

In a typical Indian meal of several dishes, this is one you can easily choose to make hot or mild, depending on the type of curry paste you use.

Serves 4

6–8 chicken thighs, skinned
100g/4oz onion
1 clove garlic
2.5cm/1" ginger, peeled
2 tablespoons vegetable oil
1 ½ tablespoons curry paste
200g can chopped tomatoes
1 tablespoon chopped coriander leaf
50g/2oz cashew nuts
1 teaspoon garam masala
small pot plain yoghurt
fresh coriander to decorate

Process the onion, garlic and ginger finely. Mix with the oil, cover and microwave to soften at PL5/Medium for 5 minutes, stirring occasionally. Stir in the curry paste and cook on High for 2 minutes.

Choose a shallow flat dish in which the thighs fit snugly. Put the spiced onion mixture into that, and stir in the tomatoes and chopped coriander. Turn the thighs in the mixture then arrange neatly and evenly in the dish. Cover and cook for 30 minutes on Medium – add 5 minutes if the thighs were refrigerated. Turn the thighs a few times to ensure even cooking.

Process the cashew nuts with the garam masala until finely chopped but not a powder. Stir into the thighs and cook on High for 1 minute. Stir in the yoghurt and heat on High for 1 minute. Leave to stand for 5 minutes before serving, strewn with chopped coriander.

Note: if you would like a wetter texture, add more tomatoes at the start or end.

Drunken chicken

A famous dish you must prepare at least a day in advance. Be absolutely certain the chicken is cooked right through to the bone. Serve chilled as a refreshing contrast to hot dishes in a Chinese meal or as a first or main course with salad in a Western meal.

Serves 4–6, more at a buffet

   4 chicken breasts on the bone, skinned
   2.5cm/1" fresh ginger peeled, sliced
   2 spring onions
   1 litre/2 pints (approximately) chicken stock
   300ml/½ pint Shao-Hsing rice wine

Put the breasts into a shallow dish in which they fit snugly without being squashed. Sprinkle with the ginger and onion. Pour on enough stock just to cover the breasts and cover with a lid. Cook on High for 3 minutes or until the liquid is simmering around the chicken. Then reduce to PL5/Medium and cook for 15-20 minutes. Leave to cool in the stock until lukewarm.

Then remove and cut or shred the chicken in large pieces, discarding the bones. Put into a serving dish, salt lightly.

Mix together the rice wine and 150ml/¼ pint of the chicken stock from the cooking dish. Pour this over the chicken and refrigerate for up to two days, turning the chicken from time to time.

Wuxi pork

Wuxi is a famed beauty spot in southeastern China. The climate which encourages its beautiful gardens is perfect for sugar cane too, and it turns up in many dishes, often unexpectedly.

Serves 4–6

   1kg/2lb boneless pork leg
   4 tablespoons granulated sugar
   6 tablespoons dark soy sauce
   4 tablespoons Chinese rice wine
   50g/2oz fresh ginger root, thinly sliced
   Chinese or sherry vinegar to finish

First make the caramel, which is the first of two secrets of this dish. Put the sugar and 8 tablespoons of water into a glass bowl, cook on PL5/Medium for 2 minutes. Stir and cook on High for 6½ minutes. Don't stir, but remove from the microwave and it will continue to darken in colour. When it is a rich dark colour (or if it starts to smoke and burn) add the soy sauce and rice wine and stir well.

Meanwhile, trim the pork of any rind but leave on all the fat. Cut into 2.5cm/1" cubes. Put into a shallow dish and add water to half the depth of the meat. Cover loosely with a plate and microwave on PL7/Medium High for 15 minutes. Drain and pat the meat clean of all debris. Return the pork to the cleaned cooking dish, add 300mls/½ pint water, the caramel and the prepared ginger. Stir and cover.

Cook on PL5/Medium for 40 minutes, or so, stirring four or five times, and checking the texture; it is easy to overcook pork, when it becomes dry. Adjust the flavour to suit with a little more soy sauce or rice wine, and then balance and point this with a little Chinese or sherry vinegar, the second and perhaps more important secret of success

Thai-poached beef fillet

Poached fillet of beef, boeuf à la ficelle, *is one of the greatest high points of French haute cuisine. Here super succulent fillet steaks are first marinated and then poach-steamed over fragrant herbs. Ask for your steaks to be cut from the thinner end of the fillet so they stand tall when stood on their cut edges. The better the fillet steak, the better the results, so don't stint.*

Serves 4

4 thick, even sized fillet steaks,
  each weighing 150g/6oz
1 tablespoon black peppercorns
8 garlic cloves
50g/2oz fresh coriander, including stalks and
  roots
250g/8oz leeks
50g/2oz shallots
50g/2oz parsley stalks
50g/2oz basil leaves
300ml/½ pint water or white wine

If your butcher will cut the steaks from a fillet which has been tied, so much the better, but this is not strictly necessary. Pound the garlic and pepper together. Put this paste into a processor with the coriander and process until smooth – note that the more stalks and roots you have the cleaner the flavour will be. Smear evenly on the steaks and allow to marinate for 4 hours or more: cool room temperature is more effective than the refrigerator. In any case, bring back to room temperature before proceeding.

Slice the leeks lengthways into quarters and cut lengthways again to make long thin strips. Chop the shallots finely, cut the parsley stalks roughly. Mix together the leeks, shallots, parsley and basil and strew evenly over the flat base of a microwave-safe casserole dish with a tight fitting lid; choose the biggest you can. Add the water or wine, cover and microwave on High for 3½ minutes. Salt lightly to taste and then arrange the four steaks evenly towards the outside of the casserole dish. Cover and microwave on High for 4 minutes. Allow to rest for 3 minutes without raising the lid, by which time they will be lightly pink in the centre.

Serve on a bed of the fragrant vegetables and herbs, with some of the stock: or go really French and serve each steak the same way in a flat soup bowl with plenty of the liquid and add a soup spoon to the setting. The recipe for sweet potato cake makes a terrific accompaniment to this dish.

Note: those with a sure touch in things Thai might add lemon grass, lime leaves, ginger or chillies, fish sauce or chilli sauce – or anything; but beware of duplicating the flavour of the sweet potato cake if you are serving that.

Southern chilli-pork meat loaf

A fast family meal with some novel twists. Pork adds a delicious sweetness and the tomato ketchup topping stays bright red. If you apply it from a squeezable bottle the opportunities for personalising or decorating are endless. It's also much more attractive served in wedges from this pie shape than the usual slices.

Serves 6 or more

500g/1lb lean minced beef
250g/8oz lean minced pork
100g/4oz onion, finely chopped
100g/4oz celery, finely chopped
50g/2oz green pepper, finely chopped
1 bay leaf
2 tablespoons Worcestershire sauce
4 tablespoons tomato ketchup
4–6 shakes Tabasco sauce
¼ teaspoon ground nutmeg
salt and pepper
100g/4oz fresh white bread crumbs
2 eggs
(optional) chopped fresh chillies

Mix together the onion, celery, green pepper and bay leaf in a small bowl. Cover and cook for 5 minutes on High. Cool slightly and remove the bay leaf. Mix the Worcestershire sauce, tomato purée, Tabasco and half the tomato ketchup, add to the onion mixture, and then mix in the eggs. Season. Mix this into the minced meats and breadcrumbs, which is easier to do by hand. Shape evenly into a microwave-safe pie dish about 22cm/8½" in diameter. Spread with the remaining ketchup. Cook on High for 12–15 minutes, moving the dish's position once or twice. Let it sit for a good 5 minutes before serving with lots of creamy mashed potato.

Spatchcocked poussins

The simplest, most succulent way to enjoy these birds. Remove the cooked skin for superior presentation and so your accompanying sauce or seasoning goes directly on to where it does most good.

Serves 2

> 2 poussins, about 400g/14oz each
> 50g/2oz butter, salt, pepper
> flavourings

Remove the trussing from each bird, cut off the leg shanks, and then cut out the backbone of each bird with poultry shears. Put the bird breast side up on to a cutting board and press firmly over the wishbone end to flatten.

Flavour the butter highly, perhaps adding such herbs as tarragon or coriander leaf if you are not serving a sauce: for a devilled, Southern flavour, add a few drops of Tabasco, some vodka and plenty of black pepper. Lift the skin over the breasts of the birds and smear the flavoured butter directly on to the flesh; pour in any liquid which has not been taken up by the butter.

Push the legs into the breast to sit nicely flat. Secure by threading a long bamboo skewer through the base of each leg, through the base of the thigh and then to the wing diagonally opposite. Cut off excess skewer.

Arrange the birds breast side out in a dish, cover lightly and microwave on a trivet on High for 10–12 minutes if they are at room temperature, longer if they have been refrigerated. Let them stand for a few minutes (whilst you cook some vegetables).

Remove the skin over the breasts and spoon on the hot buttery sauce which has escaped. Excellent with a mound of warm gingered-kumquat and walnut relish.

Note: if for some reason you have turned on the grill or barbecue, you can indeed finish the birds this way to brown and crisp the skin, in which case you may leave it on; frankly I always microwave these birds first as they are notoriously difficult to grill through.

Rice and sauces

Nice rice: a rice primer

Cooking rice in a microwave has many advantages. By using the absorption method you are retaining the maximum vitamins and flavour possible, and although it is no faster than conventional methods it is almost impossible to burn or to cook unevenly. No boring measuring either – use the same cup for both rice and liquid and you can't go wrong. But if you use a small teacup the cooking time is, naturally, going to be shorter than if you choose a big breakfast cup or a measuring cup with a 250ml/8 or 10 fl oz capacity. Unless otherwise stated, timings are based on breakfast cups, which are more or less 250ml/8 fl oz.

The technique

There's nothing to it. Put your chosen rice in a glass bowl that is at least three times bigger than the quantity of rice. To ensure you do not get boil over, smear a little butter or olive oil around the inside edge of the bowl. If you want a richer rice flavour, first cook the rice in a few tablespoons of butter or oil for a couple of minutes on High, or until each grain is glistening and slightly opaque.

To save energy and time, the cooking liquid is always hot: tap water should be as hot as possible, but freshly boiled is better; other liquids should be brought to the boil.

Add the correct quantity to the rice, stir once and cook on a trivet in the middle of the cooker. Do not stir the white rices, whatever other microwave guides advise. Once the liquid is absorbed, take from the cooker, remove whatever cover you have used, re-cover with a folded tea towel and a plate, press to seal well and let it stand for about 5 minutes, then fork over and serve, perhaps on the warmed plate.

As with conventional cookery, you will quickly adjust timings to suit your preference – some cooks, for instance, do not bother to cover white rice.

Quantities and timings

Different rices absorb different amounts of liquid. In broad terms the amount of liquid used for basic long-grain white rices should be a scant inch, about 2cms/¾" above the surface of the rice. Remember when reheating rice that the process can encourage further cooking, and so do it with restraint.

1 cup of white rice makes 2 generous main course helpings, 4 small ones.

Basic long-grain rice
1 cup rice to 2 cups liquid: cook on High for 10–12 minutes, stand 5 minutes then flavour. 1½ cups of rice will take 12–15 minutes. 2 cups from 15-18 minutes. May be reheated.

Basmati rice
1 cup rice to 1½ cups liquid: cook on High 8–10 minutes, stand 5 minutes or more and then flavour. 1½ cups of rice will take 10–12 minutes, 2 cups 12–15 minutes. May be reheated.

The best type of rice for salads or pilaus. Pilaus are traditionally steamed a long time with their ingredients but this seems to dilute much of the flavour: far better to mix in your flavouring ingredients and give it a burst in the microwave.

Remember use plenty of butter for a pilau, but if you use the rice for a salad use only oil, or the congealed butter will look horrid. A classic Middle Eastern pilau of rice cooked in a stock would include sliced dried apricots, currants and perhaps some mint; the top should be scattered with toasted pine kernels or chopped pistachios and a little sweet spice, particularly cinnamon. In the West leftovers are the usual content. That's also true of Chinese fried rice, which should be made with basic long-grain rice.

Jasmine or fragrant rice
1 cup rice to 1 or 1¼ cups liquid: cook on High 6–8 minutes, stand 5 minutes or more and then flavour. 1½ cups will take 8–10 minutes, 2 cups 10–12 minutes. May be reheated.

Brown rice
1 cup rice to 2½–3 cups liquid: begin with 2½ cups of liquid and cook on High covered with cling film or a plate for 20 to 25 minutes: may be stirred once or twice if you must; add extra liquid at any time and cook until rice is really soft. Stand 5 minutes or more and then flavour. 1½ cups brown rice will take 25–30 minutes to cook, 2 cups from 28 to 35 minutes, but in both cases you should reduce the amount of liquid slightly, starting with, say, 4 cups of liquid for 2 cups of brown rice rather than 5. Reheats well.

Wild rice
1 cup rice to 2½–3 cups liquid: cook 30–35 minutes covered with a plate or cling film, or until the liquid is absorbed and most of the grains have split and 'butterflied'. May be stirred a few times without harm if you must, and extra liquid may be added towards the end if the rice is still tough and the grains have not begun to open. Stand at least 5 minutes and then flavour – although wild rice is always better if cooked in a stock rather than plain water, and thus may be perfect just as it is. Excellent for reheating and so may be cooked well in advance. Because wild rice is chewy and richly flavoured it is usually served in smaller amounts than white rice, as an accompaniment: thus a cup will make 4–6 servings. Quality and grain size varies enormously with wild rice and some may take rather longer to cook than indicated.

Flavouring rice

If you are using delicious basmati or jasmine rice, water is all you need as a cooking liquid although a bay leaf makes an excellent and mysterious addition. Other rices benefit from the extra flavour stock gives. But why stop there? Flavouring rice is incredibly easy and makes something which might be ordinary into a speciality.

Louisiana
Cook in tomato juice, adding some chopped garlic, a little chopped red and green pepper and a few shakes of Tabasco.

Chinese pineapple
Cook in chicken or vegetable stock with a little grated fresh ginger, some chopped green pepper and chopped fresh pineapple.

Citrus
Cook in chicken or vegetable stock with the zest of an orange and lemon; add extra fresh zest to serve. Outstandingly good with poultry and fish dishes, when you might also stir in copious amounts of coarsely chopped parsley or coriander leaf.

Oriental crunch
Flavour the cooking water lightly with soy sauce (remembering it will concentrate), add crunchy chopped water chestnuts and sliced bamboo shoots; stir in toasted peanuts or cashew nuts when cooked. Bean shoots, dried fish or chilli sauce might interest you too.

Coriander lemon
Cook in stock or water with lemon zest, stir in extra lemon zest when cooked plus plenty of coarsely chopped fresh coriander leaf, and perhaps a tiny amount of raw garlic or freshly squeezed garlic juice.

Risotto

This speciality of Venice and the Veneto must be wet, with the grains lightly bound together by a sensual creamy sauce based on emulsification of butter and Parmesan cheese with the cooking stock and starch which has come from the rice. This can only be done if you break all the usual rice cooking rules and whisk the mixture like mad, oh, and use the correct type of rice, arborio of course. Use any other type of rice, or end up with separate, dry grains, and you have a pilau, not a risotto.

You do not need to cook the rice with onion if your stock is highly flavoured enough, and because the liquid is being reduced it is best not to include salt. Use the same cup for all the measurements: a 300ml/½ pint measure will ensure there is more than enough of this most delicious of all rice dishes.

Serves 2 or 3 as a main course, 4 or more as a first course. The addition of seafood, poultry or vegetables will extend its ability to gratify.

Basic recipe:

    1 large cup arborio rice
    2 generous tablespoons butter
    2 ½–3 cups good stock, plus a little extra
    75g/3oz Parmesan cheese, freshly grated
    1 or 2 tablespoons butter
    black pepper

Measure out all ingredients and then heat the stock to boiling in a measuring jug and cover. Put the rice into a 2-litre-glass bowl and top with the butter. Cook on High for 2–3 minutes, stirring once, until the rice is shining and turning opaque, but is not browning. Pour on half the stock. Cook on High for 5 minutes, or until the stock has been almost absorbed. Remove from cooker and whisk well. Pour on half the remaining warm stock, cook until stock is again almost absorbed, about 3 minutes. Whisk again and repeat with half the remaining stock, then test: the rice should retain a little resistance in each grain. If not, cook further.

    Now you must use more judgement. Remembering

that the excess liquid must combine with the cheese and butter and be seen as a sauce for the rice, judge if there is too little. If so add more warm stock, whisking as you go and keeping a definite thick glossiness to the binding sauce. At this stage, only experience can help you, not recipes. Stir in the butter and Parmesan and whisk again until the mixture is polished and unctuous: you still have the option of adding more stock to get the correct wet texture. Although usually served warm rather than hot, you can give it a quick burst in the microwave if you like. Serve at once on warm plates, perhaps with flakes of Parmesan cheese.

Variations

Any of the above flavouring suggestions for rice cookery can be used for risotto. For instance cooking in tomato juice with finely chopped peppers and Tabasco gives a fabulous risotto to serve as a main course with grilled prawns: and so on.

Such additions as finally chopped fresh vegetables, green peas, seafood and such are traditionally added just before the final cooking or they will be broken up by the whisking. As they have little chance to add flavour to the rice or to its sauce, it follows that a better-looking and more textured result comes from stirring in the prepared additions just before serving. With a microwave this means you may quickly cook your mixed vegetables to make a risotto primavera, or your seafood, whilst the risotto is resting, stir them together, and . . . Venice on a plate.

Milanese
Dissolve powdered saffron in the stock or infuse saffron threads.

Funghi porcini
Reconstitute at least 15g/½ oz dried porcini (cepes) in water or wine and add the strained liquid to the stock; stir the mushrooms into the risotto just before serving.

Minted chicken risotto
Infuse a generous handful of mint leaves in the hot stock, removing when you have a good flavour. Complete the risotto by stirring in 15 or more sliced mint leaves. Pull 1 or 2 microwaved individual chicken breasts into generous long pieces, stir half in. Serve on a base of the remaining chicken and top with toasted almond flakes and long flakes of fresh Parmesan cheese.

Wild rice salad

Serves 2 as a main course, 4 as a snack or side salad

Cook 1 cup of wild rice as above, using chicken or vegetable stock.When still warm, season if necessary and then toss with 4 tablespoons walnut oil, 1 tablespoon sherry or balsamic vinegar. And then you should add smoky flavours and sweet fruity flavours, just by themselves or with some cold chicken, turkey, ham, tongue or game bird flesh. One of my favourite combinations is:

> **1 cooked individual chicken breast, pulled into strips**
> **¼ cucumber, peeled and diced**
> **2 or more peaches, in segments**
> **(or sliced roasted red pepper)**
> **100-250g/4-8oz kabanos or Polish sausage, in cubes**

At Christmas time, turkey or goose, some pith-free orange segments, chopped celery leaf (only) and a few toasted nuts of any sort, make a great salad. Serve with a little cranberry sauce on top and some seed mustard on the side

Or use plenty of fresh lime juice rather than vinegar, cooked seafood, chopped coriander leaf, a little garlic and some Tabasco to make a deliciously refreshing oriental seafood salad, very good with hot or cold fish.

Very thinly sliced lemon grass is excellent in such mixtures.

A *source of sauces*

Sauces might have been invented for the microwave. The even heating from all sides cuts down both the time and the risk of burning or lumpiness. If sauces really are the pinnacle of cookery, then only a little experience will put you on its peak. Honest, it's that easy. The recipes may be halved for 2 or 3 people, but only reduce the microwave timings by a third.

White sauce

The basic British white sauce is not much more than flour-thickened milk, but it can be. Flavouring the milk in advance makes what the French call a béchamel, which everyone recognises as better tasting. But even a single bay leaf can make a difference. The following proportions make a good pouring sauce of thinner rather than thicker consistency. If you want a thick sauce, say for layering in a decent lasagne, increase the flour to 50g/2oz or reduce the milk to 450mls/¾ pints.

To make about 600ml/1 pint

> 50g/2oz butter
> 40g/1½oz plain flour
> 600ml/1 pint milk
> 1 bay leaf
> salt, pepper, nutmeg

Heat the butter on High for 30 seconds, stir in the flour and cook another 1 minute, stirring once if you like. Whisk in the milk, add the bay leaf and return and cook on High for 3–5 minutes depending on how cold the milk was. Whisk the mixture a couple of times throughout. Remove the bay leaf and then season the white sauce to your taste. If you can let the sauce sit for a good long while, say 15 minutes, and then zap it back to full heat with just a minute or so in the microwave the flavour will be much improved. Pouring through a fine sieve always seems to improve such sauces.

But not half as much if you take the time to do the following:

Béchamel sauce
An hour or more before you plan to make the sauce, put the milk into a jug with a stick or two of carrot, half a small onion in one piece, a small piece of celery, lots of parsley stalk, a bay leaf, some peppercorns and a small piece of lemon zest. Cover and microwave on High for 2 minutes or until the milk is rather more than hand hot but nowhere near boiling. Let it sit until cool and then strain it and use it to make your béchamel.

Cheese sauce
Add 125-200g/4–6 oz of highly flavoured cheese (not bland so-called cooking cheese), either a mature Cheddar, a Parmesan or a pecorino, for instance. A teaspoon or more of a high quality Dijon mustard and a sprinkle of nutmeg make a great difference.

Cream sauce
For rich dishes, for fish or baked pasta for instance: 600ml/1 pint single cream or half milk and half double cream.

White wine sauce
Make a thick sauce with only 300ml/½ pint milk or single cream and then whisk in white wine. Press cling film or baking paper to the surface and return to the microwave on Low for 15 minutes to let the flavours mature. Note, if you are to use this for fish, the wine used must not be a dry or elegant wine, but a medium sweet or very fruity wine. White vermouth is an excellent choice as it also contains extra flavourings. Whisk in some cream or a knob of butter to polish the sauce.

An elegant late supper dish might be medallions of monkfish or large prawns with a vermouth cream sauce on saffron rice, all made without fuss, mess, steam or noise in the microwave.

Velouté sauce

A particularly important sauce this, and one rather overlooked. Instead of being made with milk it is made with stock, and is thus an altogether tastier and lighter in fat thing, although a little cream or milk is often added to finish. Ideally use a stock related to the food with which it is being served: vegetable stock for baked courgettes, chicken stock for poached chicken, and so on. Variations are infinite, according to your taste and what you have on hand. Thus, you could make your sauce with ¾ milk and ¼ stock or half and half. Even more elegant results come from using some milk, some stock and some wine. Over to you really.

A quick egg custard

When speed is of the essence you can make an egg custard in a single container, ideally a glass jug. Here's how. Perfect for proper ice creams, too.

Serves 4 or more

    2 whole eggs
    1 tablespoon or so sugar
    few drops natural vanilla essence
    450ml/¾ pint milk or single cream

Whisk the eggs lightly with the sugar and vanilla. Then whisk in the milk and microwave on High for 2 minutes if the milk or cream was at room temperature, for 3 minutes if from the refrigerator. Whisk well and heat another minute. Once whisked you should find it beginning to thicken. Thin custards are much nicer than thick, but a few extra bursts and whisks, for no more than 30 seconds at a time should be OK. If, horrors, the sauce is thickening too much and threatens to scramble, pour in some cold milk, whisk furiously and pour it into another container.

A further 150ml/¼ pint of milk or cream, or any amount of alcohol may, of course, be used to thin the sauce further. A thin egg custard is much more correct and sophisticated than a thick one and a cognac or rum-flavoured thin custard is the proper and most infuriatingly more-ish sauce for Christmas pudding.

Creamy egg custard

There's no risk of burning or sticking when you make these delicate sauces in the microwave, and there is no direct heat to cause problems. Such sauces are noticeably thinner than custard made with powder, and all the more delicious for being so.

Serves 4

284ml carton single cream
2 egg yolks
2 level tablespoons caster sugar
vanilla essence or Bourbon

Put the cream into a large microwave-safe jug or bowl and heat on High for 3 minutes or until just boiling. Meanwhile whisk the egg yolks and the sugar together. Pour a little of the hot cream on to the egg mixture and mix well. Pour back into the hot cream and mix. Return to the microwave. Cook at PL5/Medium for 2 minutes, remove and whisk well. It should be slightly thickened, but will thicken more in the hot jug. The more sugar you have added the longer this takes to cook and thicken. Once cooled to warm and thickened a little, flavour lightly with vanilla essence, Bourbon or Southern Comfort. Serve warm rather than hot.

May be flavoured in other ways for different puddings. It is also excellent cold and the perfect base for ice creams when folded into an equal amount of lightly whipped double cream.

If your cream comes in 300ml/½ pint cartons, use all of that: if you only find double cream, dilute it with some milk.

Variations on both styles

Chocolate custard
Stir in 2–3 generous teaspoons of cocoa powder into the egg yolks and sugar or into the whole eggs if you are making a quick custard.

Bay custard
A very old-fashioned but very delicious treat. Heat the milk with 1 or 2 bay leaves and leave to macerate until a good strong flavour has developed. Particularly good with baked apples.

Foamy custard
Equally old-fashioned and very much a cheat's way to make something like zabaglione. Make a thicker creamy egg custard than usual by adding a tablespoonful of cornflour to the egg yolks. Once the custard is made, whisk up the 2 egg whites until foamy but not dry and fold them into the warm custard.

Zabaglione

However you make this frothy warm Italian speciality, it takes time and concentration. But the microwave means you are less likely to end up with scrambled eggs. Serve just as it is, the way you find in Italian restaurants, or use it as a special sauce for Christmas pudding, traditionally known in Britain as foaming sauce.

Serves 4

> 1 large egg
> 2 yolks from large eggs
> 50g/2oz caster sugar
> 150ml/¼ pint Marsala, sweet sherry or dessert
>   wine

Put the egg and the yolks, which should be at room temperature into a large clean bowl and remove any remaining threads. Whisk until creamy, and then add the sugar and continue beating until light and rather like lightly whipped cream. Traditionalists use a hand whisk and a copper bowl, but electric beaters work just as well with this method.

The alcohol used is traditionally a sweet rich wine, but sweet liqueurs can also be used, particularly the orange flavoured ones. For those with less sweet teeth naturally sweet dessert wines give a lighter cleaner finish that Marsala or sherries. Put whatever you choose into a jug and microwave on High for 1–1½ minutes, or until just beginning to bubble at the edges. Rebeat the egg mixture and pour the hot alcohol in a slow steady stream, whisking continuously. Once you see it thicken, put the mixture into the microwave on Low for about 1 minute or until the sides of the bowl feel warm. Whisk at high speed for 4–5 minutes or until the zabaglione is thick and still warm.

As a single dessert, spoon into warm stemmed glasses and serve, accompanied by sponge fingers. If serving as a sauce for steamed or other puddings (poached fruit for instance) zabaglione may be served thinner and hotter, that is with rather less final whisking.

My barbecue sauce

A really old favourite which everyone seems to like, so why change it? Make it well in advance, reheat in the microwave and then keep hot on the back of the barbecue. Or don't have a barbecue at all and use it as a marinade when you are grilling or baking anything from chops to chicken wings.

May be diluted to make up to 600ml/1 pint

2 tablespoons butter
1 tablespoon oil
150g/6oz onion, chopped
4 celery sticks, trimmed, finely chopped
1 medium green pepper, finely chopped
2-4 cloves garlic, chopped
2 tablespoons red wine vinegar
2 tablespoons lemon juice
2 tablespoons Worcestershire sauce
2 heaped tablespoons dark brown sugar
1 tablespoon mustard powder
1 teaspoon salt
300ml/½ pint tomato ketchup

Mix the butter, oil and onion in a bowl, cover and cook on High for 8 minutes or more until lightly browned. Stir from time to time and keep the onion towards the outside of the bowl so it does not burn in the centre. Add the other vegetables and cook for another 5 minutes until they are well softened. Add the liquid, sugar, mustard, salt and ketchup. Stir well, cover and cook on PL5/Medium for 15 minutes or more, until a really good thick texture. May be used as it is but is generally enjoyed more if diluted with tomato juice or water. For those who like a hotter sauce, offer Tabasco separately.

Chocolate baking

Chocolate peanut butter brownies

The moist chewiness of real brownies made extra attractive by the unexpected salty crunch of peanut butter. A winner with kids and adults alike. Unlike some microwave baking these are even better the day afterwards. Serve as they are or with ice cream.

Makes 21.5 × 16.5cm tray/approx. 9" × 7" or 6–12 pieces

100g/4oz butter
100g/4oz dark plain chocolate
200g/6oz caster sugar
2 tablespoons cocoa powder
4 eggs
1 heaped teaspoon ground cinnamon
10 tablespoons crunchy peanut butter
100g/4oz plain flour

Put the butter and broken up chocolate into a heatproof jug or bowl and heat on High for 1 minute. Stir until smooth, adding in the sugar, cocoa, cinnamon, eggs and six tablespoons of the crunchy peanut butter. When evenly blended, stir in the flour. Pour into the baking tray and dot with the remaining peanut butter.

Bake on a trivet on High for 4½ minutes, changing the position of the tray half way through. The mixture should just be set. Rest for 5 minutes, then cover with foil until cold. Good served at room temperature or lightly chilled.

Cheat's choc-mint layer cake

The fastest, gooiest, quick pudding or tea-time treat imaginable. Ring the changes by using other chocolate coated sweets.

Makes 6–8 servings

1 packet chocolate Victoria cake mix
50g/2oz butter, softened
2 eggs
3 tablespoons water
2 tablespoons cocoa powder
1 packet After Eight dinner mints

Line a glass tray 30.5 × 23cm/12" × 9" with grease proof paper. Make the chocolate cake mixture by whisking the powder supplied together with the butter, eggs and water for 2 minutes. Pour on to the paper in the tray and spread evenly. Bake on High for 3½ minutes. It may look a little moist in patches but these will disappear if you rest it for 5 minutes. Meanwhile prepare another piece of grease proof paper and sprinkle it with 2 tablespoons of cocoa powder. Turn the cooked sponge on to the sprinkled grease proof paper and remove the top grease proof.

Break the After Eight mints in half roughly and scatter evenly over ⅔ of the warm surface of the sponge.

Cut the sponge into three, cross wise, so that one third has no mints on it. Put the third with no After Eights on to the outer third, thin side to thick side so it makes as even a slab as possible. Invert the central third which should be rather thicker on to those two, so that the melting After Eights make a filling. Whilst warm, use a serrated knife to trim the ends and any of the edges which are not even. The mints should dribble and melt most pleasingly. Serve whilst warm, or within an hour or so, with plenty of cream and/or ice cream.

For a more professional look sieve a little icing sugar over the top just before serving.

Rich chocolate ring with mocha-walnut ganache

The richest chocolate cake I know, but cooked in minutes for a spectacular dessert or special tea time.

For the cake:

> 150g/6oz darkest possible chocolate
> 150g/6oz unsalted butter
> 150g/6oz caster sugar
> 100g/4oz walnut pieces
> 4 large eggs, separated
> 50g/2oz self-raising flour

For the ganache:

> 100g/4oz chocolate as above
> 284ml/10 fl oz carton double cream
> 2 heaped teaspoons instant espresso coffee
>   powder

Lightly butter a large, glass ring mould and dust with cocoa powder. For even more security when it comes to turning the cake out you might like to line the base with cooking parchment or to line the whole mould with cling film, in which case there is no need to butter and dust anything.

Break the chocolate and butter into a large mixing bowl and heat in the microwave on High for 2 minutes. Stir well until chocolate has melted, stir in the sugar and let it cool. Meanwhile scatter the walnuts on to a plate and microwave on High for 2 minutes, mix about well, push into a doughnut shape and return to microwave for another minute or more until nicely browned. Reserve a quarter of the toasted walnuts and then process the larger amount until very fine indeed.

Beat the egg yolks one by one into the chocolate mixture, also adding the processed nuts and flour.

Whisk up the whites until fluffy but not dry. Stir in a quarter to lighten the mixture and then fold together. Scoop carefully and evenly into the prepared mould. Put into the microwave on a suitable trivet and cook on High for 4½ minutes. Then let it rest in the mould for 5 minutes before turning out on to a cooling rack.

To make the ganache: break the chocolate into half the cream and warm in the microwave on High for 1 minute. Whisk until combined, stir in the instant coffee powder and then allow to cool. Stir in the remaining cream, which should be chilled. Whisk well until the mixture is light in colour and increased in volume. Spoon roughly over the cold cake; fork lightly or smooth. Top with the reserved walnuts. When the icing is set, serve on a suitable plate.

Chocolate amaretti cheesecake

For lovers of almonds. If you can find almond (rather than coconut) macaroons these do admirably, particularly as they are cheaper than Italian amaretti biscuits. The results do not seem to be so good if the biscuits are crushed too finely, so err on the side of roughness to be sure.

Makes 8–12 rich portions

For the crust:

> 100g/4oz pack amaretti or almond macaroons, roughly crushed
> 50g/2oz dark chocolate
> 50g/2oz butter

For the filling:

> 500g/1lb ricotta, curd or cream cheese
> 3 tablespoons dark rum or cognac
> 3 generous tablespoons cocoa powder
> 3 eggs
> 200g/7oz amaretti or almond macaroons, roughly crushed

For the crust: melt the butter and chocolate together for 1 minute on High. Pour on to the first measure of biscuits mix well, and press evenly into a microwave-safe flan dish of 1 litre/2 pint capacity, using the back of a spoon.

For the filling: beat the cheese with a fork to smooth it a little, and then beat in the alcohol and cocoa. Whisk together the eggs and fold into the mixture. Reserve a few tablespoons of crushed macaroons. Stir the remainder into the mixture. Taste and add up to 50g/2oz sugar if you have a particularly sweet tooth. Pour evenly into the prepared flan dish and sprinkle with the reserved macaroons. Cook on a trivet at PL5/Medium for 9 minutes. Let it cool completely and then chill before serving, with dollops of soured cream. If you can let the cheesecake cool in the microwave oven this will lessen the chance of it splitting, although this happens to me whatever I do!

Chocolate studded courgette-fudge cake

Extraordinary, but no more so than a carrot cake. This will rise well then slowly subside to increase the fudginess, becoming more the texture of brownies. Highly recommended for chocolate lovers.

For a deep ring mould 1.25 litre/2½ pint capacity

350g/12oz courgettes, finely grated
100g/4oz dark soft brown sugar
75g/3oz butter
2 eggs
1 teaspoon vanilla essence
4 tablespoons milk
250g/8oz self-raising flour
1 teaspoon cinnamon
3 tablespoons cocoa powder
100g/4oz (approx.) pack plain chocolate drops

Put the grated courgettes into a flat bottomed container and microwave uncovered on High for 2 minutes: tip on to a clean tea towel, roll up and squeeze. Unroll, mix about, roll up and squeeze again. Open the towel, spread out the courgettes and let them cool.

Line the base of the mould with baking parchment or grease proof paper, or the whole mould with cling film. Cream together the sugar and butter. Beat in the eggs, vanilla and milk. Sift together the flour, spices and cocoa powder and fold in. Fold in the chocolate drops (as some packs are larger, a few more won't matter) and then the courgettes. It will be a firm mixture, but there is more moisture in the courgettes, which they will contribute. Spoon evenly into the mould. Bake uncovered on a trivet for 9 minutes at PL5/Medium. Allow to cool and shrink for 10 minutes. Loosen well, particularly down the sides of the central tube, and turn out. For a firmer, fudgier texture cook up to 2 minutes longer. When cool, smother with Chocolate Glaze.

Particularly good served with ice cream. Improves in flavour and texture over several days.

Doubly decadent cappuccino croissant pudding

The best croissants you can buy stuffed with ricotta cheese, cinnamon and chocolate, sprinkled with rum and then baked in a light custard flavoured with espresso coffee and cream. You'll never eat bread and butter pudding again.

Serves 4–6

   3 large, day old croissants (about 175g/6oz)
   100g/4oz ricotta cheese or mascarpone
     (cultured cream)
   2 teaspoons ground cinnamon
   50g/2oz dark chocolate, roughly chopped

3 tablespoons dark rum
300ml/½ pint full milk
150ml/¼ pint (approx.) single cream
1 heaped tablespoon espresso instant coffee
50g/2oz caster sugar
4 eggs

In a large microwave-safe jug, mix together the milk, cream, coffee powder and sugar. Microwave on High for 5 minutes or until really hot. Stir well.

Meanwhile, slice the croissants in half horizontally and spread with the ricotta or mascarpone; sprinkle them with half the cinnamon and half the chocolate. Put the croissants back together again. Cut into three. Arrange in a suitable dish, round or square, into which they will fit with space to allow for expansion. Sprinkle with the rum. Break the eggs into a bowl and beat lightly. Whisk the hot milk mixture again and taste, adding more coffee or sugar; the coffee flavour should be very pronounced. Stir into the eggs and then pour on to the croissants, leave for 10 minutes or so until the croissants have swollen and taken up as much liquid as they can without dissolving completely.

Sprinkle with the remaining cinnamon and then the remaining chocolate.

Microwave on a trivet at Medium/PL5 for 6 minutes. Give the dish a half turn and cook at Medium/PL5 for another 6 minutes.

Let it rest 5 minutes before checking if it is fully set: a little runniness in the centre is preferable to it being overcooked and tough. If you are in a hurry you can use a higher power but the texture will not be as light and voluptuous. Best served warm rather than hot, and during the time you wait the custard will set further.

Ideally, let it rest until lukewarm before serving with unsweetened whipped cream or mascarpone.

Chocolate ginger mud wizardry

Comfort food gone to heaven. And no pudding has ever been more aptly named. It goes into the oven looking like a mud pool and comes out looking like a lumpy mud pool. In the meantime a sponge pudding has magically emerged, sitting in an ocean of chocolate gingery sauce.

Serves up to 6

For the pudding:

> 100g/4oz self-raising flour
> 50g/2oz dark soft brown sugar
> 1 tablespoon cocoa powder
> 1 teaspoon ground ginger
> 150ml/¼ pint milk

For the topping:

> 100g/4oz dark soft brown sugar
> 3 tablespoons cocoa
> 2 tablespoons chopped preserved ginger
> 2 tablespoons soft butter
> 300ml/½ pint milk

Mix the first amount of dried ingredients together and then stir in the milk. Put this batter evenly into a high sided microwave-safe container, about 20cms/9" wide.

Sprinkle the top with the second amount of sugar, cocoa powder and ginger. Dot with the butter and pour on the milk gently.

Cook on a trivet at PL5/Medium for 6 minutes, and then High for 2 minutes or more, until the sides are bubbling. Let it sit for 5 minutes before serving, stirring the sauce as you do to make the final mixture. Needs plenty of cream. I think whipped cream is best.

Chocolate glaze

To cover the top and sides of a single cake

100g/4oz dark chocolate
2 tablespoons double cream
2 tablespoons butter

Break up the chocolate into evenly sized pieces and heat on High for 1 minute. Stir, and if necessary heat another 20–30 seconds. Stir very well until smooth, even and glossy. Use when only just warm. there should be enough to cover an average cake with a bright glaze.

Hot chocolate sauce

Makes about 750 ml – 4–6 servings

284 ml/10 fl oz carton, double or whipping cream
150g/6oz plain chocolate
100g/4oz white or dark brown sugar
1 generous tablespoon butter
1 teaspoon vanilla
or
alcohol to taste: rum, cognac, whisky or orange liqueurs are best

Pour the cream into a large microwave-safe bowl or jug. Break in the chocolate and add the sugar: dark brown sugar gives a deeper, fudge flavour. Add the butter. Microwave on High for 7–8 minutes, or until mixture just begins to boil. It will look pretty horrid, but persevere and whisk well. When it is even, flavour to your taste, first with extra sugar if you need it, and then with vanilla or other flavourings. Best enjoyed warm rather than hot.

Note: if your cream comes in a 300ml/½ pint carton use it all.

Puddings

Poached pears in vine leaves

A traditional combination of flavours brought up to date.

Serves 6

> 3 ripe but firm pears
> 6 cardamom pods
> 4 cloves
> 1–2 cinnamon sticks
> 2–3 teaspoons clear honey
> clear apple juice
> 10–12 vine leaves, prepared

First ensure the vine leaves have been properly soaked to remove any saltiness. If you are using fresh ones, pour on boiling water, and let them sit until droopy; drain and dry. If they taste a little bitter, repeat the process once or twice more. Then halve the pears from top to bottom, peel, and then remove the core remains. Fan by cutting from the thick end almost to the stalk end.

Line a suitable flat bottomed container with vine leaves, put on a layer of pears and half the spices and honey. Put on another layer of leaves, pears spices and honey, cover with vine leaves and pour on just enough apple juice to cover. Cover the dish lightly and cook on High for 10–15 minutes or until the pears are tender. Leave for 24 hours before serving if you can.

Sri Lankan coconut cake

Stays wonderfully moist even without the syrup. Good to eat by itself but also the perfect accompaniment to tropical fruits.

Serves 6–8 or more

   100g/4oz desiccated coconut
   375ml/12 fl oz water
   2 eggs, separated
   250g/8oz caster sugar
   175g/6oz rice flour
   85g/3oz self-raising flour
   1 teaspoon baking powder
   ½ teaspoon ground cardamom
   ¼ teaspoon ground cloves
   ¼ teaspoon ground cinnamon
   1 tablespoon rose water
   50g/2oz blanched almonds, chopped

For the syrup:

   4 tablespoons rose water
   8 tablespoons water
   4 tablespoons caster sugar
   6 cardamom pods, lightly crushed

Line a 1.5 litre/3 pint ring mould with cling film or lightly oil it. Put the coconut and water into a processor or blender and process until almost a purée. Beat the egg yolks and a tablespoon of the purée with half the sugar until pale and creamy. Add the remaining purée and beat well. Sift together the flours, baking powder and spices and stir into the mixture. Mix in the rose water and nuts. Whisk the egg whites until stiff and beat in the remaining sugar until the mixture is firm and glossy. Fold into the mixture and then ladle into the prepared ring mould.
Bake on High for 7 minutes, remove and cover with

a clean tea towel for 10 minutes. Meanwhile mix together the syrup ingredients and heat at PL4 for 3 minutes. Cover and allow to brew until the cake has finished standing and then strain. Turn out the cake, prick all over and then pour the syrup evenly over it. You might like to double the amount of syrup.

Best served with tropical fruit or fruit sauce, and extra delicious if lightly chilled.

Individual summer puddings

Save time and washing up by giving the fruit a burst of heat in the microwave after making the puddings, so all the flavours and juices remain where they are needed. Exact quantities and amount will depend on the size of your ramekins. Mine are 150ml/¼ pint capacity

Serves 4

> 750g/1½ lb mixed summer fruits, or more (see note)
> 12 slices thin white bread
> 300ml/½ pint sugar-free Ribena

Lay out 8 slices of the bread, which is best a day old and use one of the ramekins to cut out 8 circles. Put one in the bottom of each ramekin and sprinkle with a generous tablespoon of the blackcurrant syrup. Use the other four slices of bread to cut thin long slices as wide as the ramekins are deep, and line each of them without overlapping the bread, which would make it too thick. Pack each ramekin really full with fruit, pressing down. Add a tablespoon more of blackcurrant syrup to each, then put on the tops and press down firmly. Arrange evenly in the microwave and cook on High for 3 minutes. Check the interiors are hot and the fruit juicy, if not give them another minute. Whilst still hot, wrap each in cling film, arrange in a square shape, put a chopping board on top and weight with cans until cold. Refrigerate stacked, changing the order from time to time.

Make a sauce by cooking the remaining fruit and Ribena for 2 minutes on High, liquidising and straining. Cool and then sweeten highly, remembering the puddings have only natural sweetening. Chill. Turn out the puddings on to individual flat plates and cover with the sauce: do this a little in advance if you can, so any remaining white patches absorb the sauce.

Note: it is best to have at least 1kg/2lbs fruit on hand; there should be a good proportion of blackcurrants as these give the classic colour and flavour. The bags of frozen summer fruits available in some supermarkets work excellently.

Sussex pond pudding

A famous old pudding rediscovered and celebrated by the late Jane Grigson. It needs to be made slightly differently, but as long as you ensure the butter and sugar are really well creamed the results are terrific. The fine grains of light soft brown sugar will cream much more easily than demerara.

Serves 4–6

  500g/1lb self-raising flour
  100g/4oz suet or cold butter
  200ml/⅓ pint (approx.) cold water
  1 thin-skinned lemon 150g/5oz
  250g/8oz demerara or light brown sugar
  250g/8oz butter, slightly warmed

Line a 1.5 litre/3 pint pudding bowl with cling film. Rub the suet or butter into the flour and make a firm pastry dough with the cold water. Chill lightly whilst you proceed. Prick the lemon all over with a thin-tined fork, put into a small bowl, cover and microwave on High for 4 minutes.
  Reserve a quarter of the dough. Roll the remainder out, fold into quarters and then line the pudding bowl evenly to just below the rim. Cream together the sugar

and butter: the sugar really must be dissolved in the butter, and this takes time.

Put ⅔ of this mixture into the prepared pudding basin. Stand the cooked lemon in the centre, adding any liquid from it. Spoon on the remaining butter/sugar. Roll out the reserved dough and make a lid, which should sit inside the rim of the bowl, with its centre resting on the top of the lemon. Join the lid and sides firmly, pressing with a fork. Put a plate over the basin. Stand on a trivet and cook on High for 10 minutes: if you are unsure of your creaming technique, cook instead on PL7/Medium High for 15 minutes, which gives the butter longer to dissolve the sugar. Rest for 5 minutes. Turn out on to a large, lipped plate. Cut carefully to release the pond of lemon flavoured, butter syrup, and serve each diner with a portion of the lemon.

Passion-fruit and apple caramel mousse

Wondrous when warm, fabulous when cold. And all because it combines the magical flavours of caramel and passion fruit.

Serves up to 6

    1kg/2lbs Golden Delicious apples
    25g/1oz butter
    100g/4oz caster sugar
    85g/3oz ground almonds
    pulp of 8 passion-fruits
    4 medium eggs
    50g/2oz sugar
    6 tablespoons orange juice
    2 tablespoons butter

Core, segment and peel the apples. Chop roughly. Put into bowl, cover and microwave on High for 8–10 minutes or until really soft. Mash well, adding the butter, caster sugar, almonds and passion-fruit pulp. Whisk the eggs and beat them in evenly.

Choose a straight sided soufflé bowl 15cm/6" diameter. Into the base put the second amount of sugar and the orange juice. Stir well and add the butter. Microwave on High for 5 minutes: the caramel should be bubbling and quite dark brown. Protecting your hands with a thick cloth, swirl the caramel evenly around and up the sides of the bowl.

Let the caramel cool just long enough to ensure it stays where it has swirled. Spoon in the prepared apple mixture. Cook covered on a trivet at PL5/Medium for 10–12 minutes, ideally moving the position of the bowl at least once. Let it cool until just warm and then turn out.

Serve with chilled whipped cream lightly flavoured with an orange liqueur.

Poached peaches and summer fruit sauce

A half bottle of a luscious sweet wine and a good peach are hard to beat, but this will do it.

Serves 4

   4 ripe firm peaches, halved
   4 cardamom pods
   2 cinnamon sticks
   8 tablespoons sweet Muscat wine
   8 tablespoons (approx.) mixed summer fruits

Arrange the peaches cut side down in a suitable container (a round one is best), pour on the sweet white wine and arrange the fruit evenly in the spaces between the fruit. Cover with cling film or a plate and cook on High for 7–12 minutes depending on how big or ripe the peaches are.

Remove the peaches and push the juices and fruit through a sieve. Serve the peach halves surrounded by some of the sauce, hot or cold. Wonderful with ice cream, of course.

Pecan-butterscotch banana pudding

Turn this out, pour on the butterscotch sauce, and then dare to eat it. So sinful it has to be good.

Serves 6–8

The pudding:

>   50g/2oz butter
>   100g/4oz caster sugar
>   2 medium eggs
>   250g/8oz very ripe banana flesh
>   1 tablespoon milk
>   150g/6oz self-raising flour

The sauce:

>   250g/8oz light brown sugar
>   small carton double cream
>   50g/2oz butter
>   50g/2oz pecan or walnut pieces

Combine sauce ingredients in a large glass bowl. Cook on High for 3 minutes, stirring from time to time. The sauce will begin to boil and emulsify into the conventional creaminess. When this happens, pour half into the base of a lightly buttered 1.5 litre/3 pint ring mould and scatter with the nuts.

Cream the butter and sugar together really well, and then beat in the eggs. Mash the bananas roughly and stir in with the milk. Incorporate the flour evenly, but do not over-beat. This can be done in a processor. Spoon evenly into the mould and cook on High for 4½ minutes. Allow it to rest for a few minutes whilst you reheat the remaining butterscotch sauce. Turn the pudding out on to a large plate. Serve in wedges and pass the sauce separately. Vanilla ice cream is a terrific foil and complement to the flavours and textures.

Date-pecan bread pudding with creamy custard sauce

A classic of the Southern States, and yet not too different from Britain's standby.

Serves 6–8

350g/12oz day-old French bread (country-style
  rather than stick if possible)
450ml/¾ pint full cream milk
50g/2oz butter
100g/4oz dark brown soft sugar, plus 2
  tablespoons
4 eggs
2 teaspoons ground cinnamon
1 teaspoon real vanilla essence
100g/4oz chopped dates or seedless raisins
50g/2oz pecans or walnuts, roughly chopped

The bread may have its crusts on. Process into crumbs, pour on the milk and let it stand a few minutes or until the two can be beaten to smoothness. Soften the butter for 10 seconds in the microwave on High. Mix together the eggs, sugar, melted butter, cinnamon and vanilla essence and beat into the bread mixture. Stir in the chopped dates or seedless raisins. Pour into a microwave-safe dish about 20cm x 16cm/9" × 7". Sprinkle on the extra 2 tablespoons of dark brown sugar and the pecans.

Cook uncovered on a trivet at PL5/Medium for 12–15 minutes or until the centre is lightly risen and a knife comes out cleanly. It is important to change the position of the tray a few times, say every 5 minutes. Let it cool for 10–15 minutes, and then serve with a hot custard sauce (see sauces section).

Hazelnut carrot cake

Nuts and carrots are both used to give a rich moistness to cakes, but here they are combined for guaranteed goodness. This recipe using oil rather than butter is common in carrot cakes and is also quicker than butter.

225ml/8fl oz vegetable oil
250g/8oz soft dark brown sugar
3 eggs
275g/9oz self-raising flour
2 teaspoons ground cinnamon
250g/8oz carrot, finely grated
100g/4oz hazelnuts, chopped

Arrange the hazelnuts in a hollow ring shape on a flat plate and microwave on High for 3 minutes, mix well, rearrange into the ring shape again and microwave in bursts of 1 minute until lightly browned. Cool.

Put the oil, sugar and eggs into a bowl and beat well until thoroughly combined and the sugar is dissolved: don't use demerara or other course-grained sugars. Mix together the flour, and cinnamon, then stir into the first mixture. Fold in the carrots and the hazelnuts.

Spoon into a deep microwave cake ring of 1 litre/2 pints capacity.

Cook on a trivet on Medium for 10 minutes or until just shrinking from the edges but slightly damp on top. Stand for 5 minutes and then turn on to a wire rack to cool.

If you like cakes with syrup poured through them, rather than going to the bother of icing or decorating, mix together a generous 150ml/¼ pint of fresh orange juice, plus a tablespoon of lemon or lime juice, and 100g/4oz of caster sugar (or to taste). Microwave on High for about 3 minutes or until the caster sugar is dissolved. Let it cool slightly and spoon over the cake. Of course, whipped cream, orange zest, and more toasted hazelnuts wouldn't hurt the look or the taste.

Spotted dick

It's not the real thing unless it is cooked in a sausage shape. The microwave cooks this famous pudding in less than a tenth of the usual time, but because it is steamed in paper and cloth which inhibits its ability to rise fully, you get the traditional firm texture that is so loved – or hated. Using water rather than milk is also authentic, but most people these days will prefer the softer texture given by milk. Must be served with custard. Oceans of it.

Serves 4–6

> 100g/4oz butter or suet
> 200g/6oz caster sugar
> 2 eggs
> 300g/9oz self-raising flour
> 2 tablespoons water or milk
> 100g/4oz currants

Before you begin, choose a spotlessly clean tea towel, rinse it quickly in cold water and ring out so it is evenly damp. Lay it on a large flat plate which will go into your microwave. On the cloth put a piece of non-stick microwave or other baking paper that is about two thirds its length: cling film can be used but it is harder to use and inhibits rising rather more. Set to one side.

Combine the currants and water or milk and microwave on High for 1 minute. Let it cool while you cream together the butter and the sugar and then beat in the eggs. Fold in half the flour and then mix in the currants and all their liquid. Add the rest of the flour and mix until you have a smooth, firm but light dough, rather like a scone mixture. Don't be afraid to add a *little* more flour.

Turn the mixture on to the middle of the prepared paper and using floured hands shape into a roll no more than 15"/35cm long. Fold up the two long sides of the paper to prevent the dough spreading, and then lift the two short ends and fold down to make a crease along the top: give the pudding some free space under the crease, say 50cm/2". It might appear a little flat at this stage. Now fold the dampened tea towel over the pudding and tuck firmly under the side of the mixture. You should now have a sort of sausage shape: the loose fold of the paper and the arrangement of the tea towel will allow some rising of the mixture but not so much you would get a sponge pudding. Microwave on a trivet on Medium for 10 minutes. Press lightly using the back of a spoon and if the centre is still soft, cook on at Medium in bursts of 2 minutes. Allow to rest at least 5 minutes and then take to the table on its cooking platter, and then unwrap and reveal it there.

Syrup pudding

The top favourite basic. Quickly and easily adaptable. When you want a change from golden syrup, use maple syrup, jam, puréed fruits – or nothing at all. The sponge can be flavoured with chocolate or coffee, studded with currants, flecked with grated orange, lemon or lime zest. But you'll always come back to the original.

Serves 4–6

100g/4oz butter (or suet)
100g/4oz caster sugar
2 eggs, beaten
250g/8oz self-raising flour
(up to) 150ml/¼ pint of milk
3 generous tablespoons golden syrup
(extra) 50g/2oz butter, chopped

Lightly butter a 1 litre/2 pint pudding basin and add the golden syrup plus the extra 50g/2oz of chopped butter.

Cream the butter and sugar very well and then beat in the eggs one at a time. Fold in the flour and then enough milk to achieve a soft dropping consistency: it is better to err on the side of too soft than too firm.

Spoon the mixture into the basin, cover lightly with cling film or leave uncovered. Cook on High until well risen and just coming away from the sides, about 5 minutes: if you have the time you get an even lighter result by cooking at Medium for 8–10 minutes or until done. Let it rest for at least 5 minutes and then turn out on to a warmed platter to serve. Extra golden syrup and butter can be melted and warmed in the microwave for serving.

Variations: if you want to use suet, stir the suet, sugar and flour together, then stir in the eggs and the milk. Ground ginger is a good addition, either to the sponge or to the syrup and butter sauce.

Sticky date pudding

An absolute winner, served as a hot pudding in winter, or as the most sensationally delicious cake in summer. Conclusive proof that anyone who thinks microwave baking is dry is really missing out. And that's before you add any sauce!

Serves 6 or more

> 250g/8oz chopped dates
> 225ml/8floz water
> 1 teaspoon bicarbonate of soda
> 50g/2oz butter
> 200g/6oz caster sugar
> 2 eggs
> 200g/6oz self-raising flour

Sticky toffee sauce

> 225g/7oz soft dark brown sugar
> 300ml/½ pint double cream
> 200g/6oz butter

Reserve a couple of tablespoons of dates. Put the remainder into a bowl with the water, cover with a plate and microwave on High for 4 minutes. Stir in the soda and stand for 5 minutes before processing into a smooth purée.

Meanwhile cream the butter and sugar well and then beat the eggs one by one. Fold in the flour mixture and then the date mixture. Put the reserved dates into the bottom of a microwave ring mould 20cm/8" wide with a 1 litre/2 pint capacity. Spoon in the mixture and then cook on a trivet on High for about 5 minutes or on Medium for up to 10 minutes. Let it rest for another 10 minutes before serving, turned out.

Combine the sauce ingredients in a bowl and microwave on High for 3 minutes, stirring until the sugar is dissolved and the ingredients have amalgamated. Pour some over the pudding and pass the rest. If you would like to make the pudding in advance, let it cool and before serving, pour about a quarter of the sauce over the top and microwave on High for just 1 minute.

If serving as a cake, let it cool on a wire rack. It doesn't really need any of the sauce, but if you made up just half or quarter the amount and poured that into the cold cake . . .

Refrigerator cookies

Refrigerate the mixture, it keeps for weeks, so all you have to do is slice and bake. A basic recipe which can be varied at will. It's worth taking note of what you do and the results the first time, because every microwave is different – you might need extra flour for a firmer mixture, a little milk for a softer one. But you can't go far wrong.

100g/4oz butter
85g/3oz caster sugar
85g/3oz dark or light soft brown sugar
1 egg
½ teaspoon vanilla essence
250g/8oz self-raising flour
(up to) 250g/8oz chunky additions – see method

Cream the butter and sugars well and then beat in the egg and essence. Stir in the flour evenly.

The additions can be simply chopped glacé cherries or ginger, nuts or currants, chocolate or caramel pieces. The nicest way is to have a mixture, so each bite tastes different. Whatever you choose, mix half into the mixture and reserve the rest.

The mixture should be firm enough to roll and hold its shape. Make a roll about 40cm/15" long and wrap tightly in cling film and then with foil. Refrigerate well, at least an hour.

Cut into rounds about 1 cm thick. As the mixture spreads when cooking, 4–6 is probably the maximum to cook at one time, depending on the size of your cooker. Arrange the cookies in as big a circle as possible on non-stick baking or microwave paper on a flat plate. Sprinkle each one with a little of the reserved flavouring mixture.

Cook on High for 2–3 minutes. They will still be soft and should be slightly moist on top. Use a spatula to put the cookies on to a cooling rack, where they will crispen as they cool. It's really worth taking the time to test one batch: let them cool, taste and then perhaps adjust the mixture or cooking time. Once you get it right you'll be microwaving cookies forever with never another thought.

Especially good as an accompaniment to ice cream, but even better when they are broken up and put into ice cream. Chocolate and ginger ones are especially good in a banana ice cream, making what I call banana cookies and nice cream.

Banana ice cream

Another absolute basic. The mixture of condensed milk and cream will hold up to 300ml/½ pint of any thick fruit purée. It's also a cheat's recipe, as the result looks and tastes as though you have gone to all the bother of making a traditional custard.

Makes about 500ml/1 pint

1 small can of sweetened condensed milk,
  chilled (approx. 200ml/6fl oz)
150ml/¼ pint (approx.) carbon double cream
3 very ripe bananas, mashed
5 drops vanilla essence
2 teaspoon lemon or lime juice

Beat the sweetened condensed milk in a chilled bowl until thickening. Add the cream and keep beating until doubled in volume: for even greater yield you can actually double the amount of cream.

Fold in the bananas, vanilla essence and citrus juice, perhaps swirling rather than distributing evenly. Spoon into the container and freeze. Does not need to be rebeaten but may be after about an hour when the sides are frozen.

Roughly broken refrigerator cookies make a great addition – truly having your cookies and eating them too. Remember to soften slightly before serving.

Rocky road

This super chunky confection even looks wicked. Dark or milk chocolate hiding hunks of nuts, marshmallows and glacé cherries. If you want to serve it as a sweet snack, make it very rough with rather big pieces of the ingredients. But to include it in an ice cream, it is best made with smaller pieces and allowed to set in a thinner layer. Milk chocolate gives a sweeter but softer effect when frozen.

Makes just over 450g/1lb

350g/12oz dark or milk chocolate
50g/2oz mixed marshmallows
85g/3oz pecan nuts, roasted and coarsely
  chopped
85g/3oz glacé cherries

Break up the chocolate into even pieces, put into a
bowl and then microwave on High for 1 minute. Stir
the chocolate with a scrupulously clean and dry spoon
and microwave for another minute. Stir until smooth.
Mix in the other ingredients, stir well and turn on to
non-stick baking or microwave paper. If you think your
marshmallows are too big, cut with lightly oiled scis-
sors. Pile the mixture thickly and roughly or smooth it
out, according to use. Let it set well before breaking or
chopping up roughly.
Excellent in coffee-Tabasco ice cream. Stir in as much
or as little of the broken pieces as you like before
freezing.

Coffee-Tabasco ice cream

*Two unusual things here. First the method, which gives a
terrifically light mixture, which does not need a second beating. And then the inclusion of a light chilli bite. It sounds
surprising, and is, but used with discretion chilli gives a
truly delightful and refreshing tingle which balances the
sweetness of ice cream.*

Makes about 1 litre/2 pints

4 eggs, separated, room temperature
100g/4oz caster sugar
300ml/½ pint of double cream, lightly whipped
2 tablespoons coffee and chicory essence
2 tablespoons coffee liqueur, cognac or dark rum
4–6 shakes Tabasco to taste

Beat the egg whites until soft and peaky but not dry.

Continue to beat as you add in the sugar and beat until it is well dissolved. Whisk the egg yolks until good and frothy. Mix them with the coffee essence, the liqueur and just 4 shakes of Tabasco. Gently fold into the egg whites until evenly distributed. Taste, and add extra Tabasco if you like or dare.

Spoon into a large container and freeze. If you have the time a second beating is worthwhile after 2 hours or when still partly frozen. And if you do this the second beating is the time to add the Rocky Road if desired. Soften slightly before serving.

Note: you can use other chilli sauces, including the thicker sweet chilli sauces of Chinese cooking.

Real plum pudding

The traditional plum pudding served at Christmas time has it roots in the customs of Middle Eastern cookery, brought back to Europe by the Crusaders. Once it was virtually a soup, thick with prunes and other dried fruits and I think we should keep and enjoy some reference to its first, sticky texture. It has a wonderfully rich golden colour with a truly fabulous flavour, and a clean finish from the puréed orange and lemon. It will be much darker if you can let the fruit mixture sit overnight and make the pudding in advance: but even if you make and eat them on the same day you'll never want or need to buy plum pudding ever again!

**Makes 2 puddings each of which will serve 6–8.
Start 24 hours earlier if you can.**

350/12oz stoned ready-to eat prunes
250g/8oz seedless raisins
250g/8oz currants
100g/4oz mixed peel
50g/2oz slivered or chopped almonds
1 sharp-tasting apple
1 small orange

½ lemon
250g/8oz dark brown sugar
150g/6oz beef suet or butter
3–4 tablespoons treacle or molasses
2 tablespoons orange flower water
1 tablespoon ground mixed spice
½ nutmeg, freshly grated
¼ teaspoon ground cloves
6 tablespoons cognac or rum
150ml/5fl oz stout
250g/8oz self-raising flour
100g/4oz ground almonds
4 eggs, beaten

Roughly chop the prunes which must be the soft ready-to-eat type, and mix with the raisins and currants. Add the mixed peel and slivered almonds. Grate in the apple, skin and all. Quarter the orange and lemon and remove all pips. Cut up roughly and then liquidise, skin, flesh and all. Add this to the mixture and then add the sugar, suet or butter (chopped), the treacle or molasses, the orange flower water and the spices. Pour on the alcohols, and then stir very well indeed. Cover and microwave on High for 6 minutes. Stir well, cover again and leave to cool, ideally overnight.

Mix together the flour and the ground almonds and stir well into the mixture. Keep stirring as you work in the eggs and then stir some more, perhaps letting everyone have a stir and a secret wish.

Put a disc of buttered grease proof or silicone baking paper at the bottom of two lightly buttered 1 litre/2 pint bowls. Divide the mixture evenly between the two bowls and then seal with cling film, but do not pierce it.

Cook both puddings at the same time for 30 minutes on PL5/Medium turning each bowl through a quarter turn every 10 minutes. Do not open or pierce, as when the film cools and shrinks on to the surface this helps prevent mould appearing. Let cool and store in a cool place. If this is to be for more than a week, add extra layers of cling film.

Note: If you want to make only one pudding, or can only fit one pudding into your microwave at a time cook a single pudding for 20 minutes on Medium.

On Christmas Day reheat without removing or changing the cling film while you are enjoying your main course: a single pudding for 10 minutes on Medium: two will take 15 minutes. You should let them sit 10 to 20 minutes (they will still be boiling hot) while you prepare the sauce below, which is a more authentic accompaniment than hard sauce or brandy butter.

Then turn out on to a plate with a deep lip. Flame if you like and cut with a serrated knife, first in half and then into servings.

Frothy Victorian pudding sauce

Save the egg yolks from your Christmas snow log for this lovely light sauce. Any wine, sherry, spirit or liqueur can be used for this: a white wine gives a very light flavour, sweet sherries or orange liqueurs give the richest sauces.

Serves 6–8

> 6 egg yolks
> 100g/4oz caster sugar
> 6 generous tablespoons cream
> ½ teaspoon vanilla
> 6 tablespoons wine, sherry, spirit or liqueur
> freshly grated nutmeg

Cream together the egg yolks and the sugar and then microwave on High for 45 seconds. Stir in the cream, vanilla essence and alcohol and microwave on High for 90 seconds more. Whisk vigorously until thickened, put into a warm bowl, grate on the nutmeg and then serve whilst still hot and frothy.

Chocolate dipped cherries

A simple way to keep children quiet – they can make them quite safely – and then the keep adults quiet as they eat them. Strawberries, physalis, anything with stalks and stems, can also be used.

100g/4oz darkest possible chocolate
50g/2oz unsalted butter
1 tablespoon cream, port, sherry, cognac or rum

Chop the chocolate and butter and put into a jug with the chosen liquid. Microwave on High for 2–4 minutes, stirring from time to time. Let it cool for the same amount of time. Then dip the fruits, one by one, putting them on to baking paper until set. A very light sprinkle of icing sugar (through a fine sieve) gives a very festive extra touch. Chocolate fruit is perfect for decorating your Christmas snow log.

Christmas snow log

Essentially, this is the great Australasian Pavlova cake in a different guise. It's cooked in layers with cinnamon and cocoa, so it looks like a real log with age rings, and then filled with tangy lemon curd and topped with cream and nuts for a frosted bark look. Great fun and great tasting too.

Serves 6 or more

> 6 egg whites
> 250g/8oz caster sugar
> 2 teaspoons cornflour
> 2 teaspoons vinegar
> 1 teaspoon vanilla essence
> 2 teaspoons cocoa powder
> 1 teaspoon ground cinnamon
> 100g/4oz chopped almonds or hazelnuts
> extra tablespoon caster sugar
> 2–4 tablespoons top quality lemon or orange
>   curd
> 300ml/½ pint double cream, whipped

Line an oblong sponge roll tray of 30cm x 20cm/12" × 8" with silicone baking paper, making an upturn all round of at least 2.5cm/1": snip the paper down to the base at the corners so it fits neatly.

Using an electric beater, begin whisking the egg whites and once foamy, slowly add half the sugar, beating all the time. Once good and glossy, stir in the remainder and beat just a short time. Fold in the cornflour, and then the vinegar and vanilla essence. Mix the cocoa powder and cinnamon together and put into a fine sieve.

Spread one third of the mixture evenly into a prepared tray. Sprinkle evenly but lightly with a third of the cocoa and cinnamon mixture: cinnamon. Add another third of the mixture and sprinkle that with half the remaining cocoa and cinnamon mixture. Spread on the last third but do not sprinkle it. Stand on a trivet and cook on High for 3 minutes.

Whilst it cools, toast the almonds or hazelnuts, arranging them in doughnut ring shape and beginning with 2 minutes on High. Mix lightly, reshape into a doughnut and toast in 30-second bursts until they are lightly golden. Let it cool and then mix with the remaining cocoa cinnamon mixture plus a tablespoon of caster sugar, a bit more if you like. Press this evenly into the top of the cooked meringue, and cover with baking paper, leaving a good margin all round.

Once the meringue is cool, put a large board or plate on top and invert the lot. Remove the top paper (originally in the bottom of the baking tray). Use a paper towel to blot up any excess moisture and then turn the board so that you are faced by one of the short ends of the meringue. Starting close to you, spread two thirds of the meringue with a thin layer of lemon or orange curd; if it is a firm commercial curd, stir in a little cream to loosen it. Roll the meringue firmly, using the paper to help you, but keeping it out of the way. Once rolled, tuck the paper underneath to keep the shape firm and then chill well, 4 hours at least. To serve, use a large sharp knife to trim the ends flat to reveal the pattern of rings: if you like trim one other at a thin, acute angle and put this on to the side of the log to look like the cut end of a branch. Spread the whipped cream on to the nut encrusted surface only, and then draw a fork through that to reveal the nuts and mix some of them into the cream, so it really does look like bark with snow on it. Some of the cream may drip over the cut surface. Chill again.

May be made a day in advance, but the nuts will soften slightly: much better made and eaten on the same day. If the cocoa smears the cut surface when you serve, run the sharp edge of a knife over the surface to clean it. Good served with a Moroccan orange salad, slices of pithless orange segment, cinnamon and a sprinkle of seasonal orange flower water.

Note: if your microwave will not take a baking dish this big, reduce everything by a half.

Christmas berry soup

Lightly thickened fruit soups are a Scandinavian invention and make a sharp and refreshing alternative to heavy hot Christmas pudding. May be served warm and slightly liquid, but it is best served lightly chilled as a lollopy soft jelly. Don't add sugar other than the fine layer used to prevent a skin forming, but rely on the sweetness of the fruit and the wine.

Serves 6

> 450ml/¾ pint sweet white wine
> 750g/1½lb mixed berries (frozen may be used)
> 2 big fresh bay leaves
> 1 cinnamon stick
> 1 generous tablespoon cornflour or arrowroot
> 6 teaspoons caster sugar

The best berries, if you have the choice, are raspberries, blueberries, blackberries and blackcurrants; a mixture of the first two is ideal.

Put the berries (defrosted if using frozen) into a large bowl and pour on the wine. Add the bay leaves and the cinnamon. Cover and microwave for 4–6 minutes, or until the wine is hot and the berries are giving up their colour; the time will depend on how cold the berries and wine were.

Slake the cornflour or arrowroot with a further 2 tablespoons of wine or of water, stir in evenly and then microwave on High in bursts of 1 minute or less until the mixture has cleared and thickened slightly. Be careful not to break up the fruit when you are stirring. Spoon into individual glasses or bowls and sprinkle lightly with caster sugar. Chill, but remove from the refrigerator at least 15 minutes before serving, so they are only just below room temperature, which accentuates the fruity sweetness. Serve with a chilled glass of the same wine used to make the soup.

Index